GOD'S CALL IS UNIQUE. For Adriaan ... ~~~ ~~~ Bijl, it was a "little bundle of sticks" given to him by some men from the remote Nduga tribe in Papua, Indonesia. Little did Adriaan know that this bundle of sticks was to become his mantle of ministry.

A.B. Simpson declared that the C&MA stands for a commitment "to reach the most neglected fields, to avoid the beaten tracks of other labourers, to press on to the regions beyond and instead of building upon another man's foundation to preach the gospel where Christ has not been named." Adriaan took this declaration to heart.

The prophet Elisha was presented with a daring choice when his mentor and spiritual father, Elijah, was taken up to heaven. The mantle of leadership fell from Elijah's shoulders to the ground in front of Elisha. All heaven held its breath. Would he pick it up? Elisha did, and a double portion of God's Spirit was poured out on him.

Adriaan van der Bijl and his wife, Mijo, were presented with a bundle of sticks—a mantle of ministry to the Nduga mountain people. The question was, "Would they pick it up?" This book is a resounding yes. They have left a legacy of transformed lives and a courageous call to future generations.

What is your bundle of sticks? Will you pick it up?

Dr. David Hearn
President of the C&MA in Canada

LAST CUCUMBER ON THE VINE is essential reading for those wanting to understand how to serve their generation well. In our comfort-loving, security -conscious world, the van der Bijl story represents their commitment and the commitment of their coworkers to give themselves wholeheartedly to God and his work. Their faithful witness away from the limelight and inundated with challenges and oppositions incarnated God's love for the Ndugas.

In a day when we often forsake dreams because of our unwillingness to risk, *Last Cucumber on the Vine* is a reminder that God places us on this earth to write a distinctly personal script for our lives. Our times call for a new generation who long for a kind of forgotten courage to live intentionally and to generate our own God-given stories.

Dr. Charles A. Cook
Professor of Global Studies and Mission
Ambrose University

IN 1887, C&MA FOUNDER, A.B. SIMPSON and Robert Jaffray, C&MA mission strategist, shared the same vision—to establish a missionary base in Dutch New Guinea. When F.G. Wissel, a Dutch aviator, spotted a network of lakes, villages, and gardens in the western highlands during a 1936 flight, Jaffray knew the time had come.

C&MA personnel made their first trip into the interior in December 1938. World War II necessitated their withdrawal until October 1946. A short time after the war ended, missionaries from Holland, Canada, and the United States arrived to introduce the gospel to the people.

Today, we estimate that 100,000 people gather together each week in some 470 C&MA churches in Papua. Because of the obedience of hundreds of missionaries from various mission agencies, and the financial and prayer support of thousands of Christ followers, *Operation World* reports this island of eight million people is 95% Christian (25% Evangelical), with twelve Bible translations and 210 New Testaments in tribal languages. Literacy is at 57%

Dr. Ron Brown
Missions Coach, CMA-Canada

IT IS THE GOSPEL STORY ALL OVER AGAIN! In the first chapter of Acts, God's messengers stepped into a world of multiple cultures, languages, and religions to tell people about Jesus. Amazing miracles happened, again and again!

Fast forward from the first century to 1960. God called Adriaan and Mijo van der Bijl to be his messengers to a remote tribe living deep within the towering mountains of Papua, just as he chose Paul, Silas, Priscilla, and Aquila in the Book of Acts.

When Adriaan and Mijo were appointed by the C&MA leadership to work with the Nduga (n-doo-gwah) tribespeople, God was already working miracles preparing the Ndugas to receive his joyful story. Adriaan and a team of four discovered that these people were hungry to learn about unending life. As the people listened to the gospel story, they realized that Jesus was the source of eternal life. It was the message they had been waiting for and a message that they eagerly shared with other tribal groups. Here begins a new chapter in the historical account of the Apostles of the Kingdom. This story about the transformation of the Nduga people will bless you as you read.

Rev. John D. Ellenberger
Damal Missionary Translator

Last Cucumber on the Vine

Last Cucumber on the Vine

The story of Adriaan van der Bijl
and the transformation
of the Nduga people

Richard Reichert
with Lorraine Willems

Three E Publishing House
Saskatoon, Saskatchewan

BV
3427.
R17
2019

Printed in the United States of America

ISBN: 9781080245123
Imprint: Independently published

For Mijo,
who never lost her focus,
her love for Mapnduma,
and her desire to live there.
1935-1986

CONTENTS

FOREWORD

THE STORY TOLD IN THIS BOOK ignites a longing to reflect on one's life and on how we prepare for tomorrow. The way the main characters acted, in times of joy and sorrow, can serve as a model for when we face important decisions. What was their compass, how did they use it and what can we learn from them when we must choose a direction?

Following Adriaan, Mijo and Elfrieda on their life's journey has this mirror effect. Again, and again, it makes you wonder, what would I have done in this or that situation? More importantly, it makes you wonder what it was that made them tick. I recommend this story, not just because it gives an intriguing picture of the past, but especially because it has the potential to impact the reader's future path. The apostle Paul invited his readers to follow his example as he followed the example of Christ. Likewise, there is much to learn from Adriaan and Elfrieda.

Their example is important in a time when the world is becoming less stable and when many feel insecure and afraid. Even Christians are tempted to give priority to protect what they have, close the gates, and guard their comfort zone.

The van der Bijls exemplify a career marked by a different perspective. It reminds us of how the apostle Paul described his motivation in Romans 15:20—It has always been my ambition to preach the gospel where Christ was not known. It was the same ambition that took Adriaan and Elfrieda to Ndugaland. It's this ambition that is needed to get new generations to reach the many people groups that are outside the realm of any church in our times.

In 1998 I had the privilege of visiting Adriaan and Elfrieda and participating in the farewell party the Ndugas organized for them. At the time, I was director of CAMA-Zending, the Alliance sending agency in the Netherlands and I travelled in the company of Pineke Renger-Ubbink and her husband, Gerard. Pineke had been a missionary herself, working on the same island from 1959 till 1963. It was a humbling experience for me to be greeted and treated as Adriaan's boss. True, I was not inexperienced, having lived in Congo for ten years, but it seemed nothing compared to what God had accomplished through these international workers in this area.

I will never forget how Adriaan walked on slippery slopes as nimble as a mountain goat, jumping from one stone to another. He was much older than I was but seemed to have so much more energy. Standing on a mountaintop, we saw a wonderful panorama, and in the vast jungle, we saw certain spots where trees were cut to erect small churches and clinics as markers of God's Kingdom making its way into the darkness.

Since then this image often came back to me while visiting many areas around the globe where there is hardly any light of the gospel, areas that need people like Adriaan and Elfrieda and through them God can bring change so that one day those areas may also be penetrated by the Kingdom of God.

I will resist the temptation to share further details. Just keep reading. There is so much more, and it is so eloquently worded! Let me give just one quote from chapter seventeen as an appetizer:

"Many times, in telling his story, Adriaan insisted that this story was bigger than him. It was about the God to whom we must give the glory for orchestrating the entrance of the Nduga people into the Kingdom of God."

Let's celebrate these remarkable people. May their example inspire us to dedicate our lives to sharing the gospel and giving glory to God!

Arie M. Verduijn

Director of CAMA-Zending—1992-2004

and President of the Alliance World

Fellowship—2004-2016

PREFACE

I FIRST MET ADRIAAN VAN DER BIJL when he was the other side of eighty, retired in an unassuming small city on the bald western prairies of Canada. Saskatoon, Saskatchewan is known more for its winters than anything else. Everything about his life would suggest that he should be uneasy in this sedentary setting, but there was a restfulness about his demeanour belying the rugged lifestyle and roughhewn existence that had marked his days. Here was a man at peace with himself.

There was a kind sparkle to his voice, an inescapable twinkle in his eye. It contradicted the stresses and trauma that had ravaged his body and mind in the climaxing days of his cross-cultural international career. Here is the story of a man who set out with a singular vision to contact and live with the Nduga mountain people of Papua, Indonesia. He saw it as his calling and vocation. It drove him to sacrificial extremes. In the end, the vision consumed him. But not before he had planted a foothold for the name of Christ among the Nduga people and established an indigenous church that survived and thrived after he was gone. His presence among the Nduga people changed its people and their worldview forever. The subhead on the cover is unapologetically and unreservedly chosen—The Story of Adriaan van der Bijl and the transformation of the Nduga people. And Adriaan would be quick to add a transformation that was only possible through a living encounter with the Redeemer King, Jesus Christ.

As Adriaan pointed out his albums to me, he seemed conflicted. He wanted to tell his story, but he was not sure anyone would want to hear it. I was struck by the humility and grace of the man and decided that it was a story that must be told.

The hard work had been done. A life had been poured out. A diligent listener named Lorraine Willems had transcribed Adriaan's story faithfully into 187 pages of text she called Tracings. There was a lifetime of photos and transparencies.

The story is not exactly chronology. I chose to highlight the pivotal moment of Adriaan's life first. His decision to seek out the Nduga people and intentionally locate his family among them was the critical decision of his life. We could view the trek into Mapnduma as the most transcendental moment of his life, and so we begin there. From that opening chapter, we go back to fill in the pieces of how Adriaan got to Mapnduma and forward from that moment to chronicle the threads of his amazing God-led life.

Men who tackle hidden valleys and steep passages are always in danger of falling off the edge. If Adriaan had not come, no one would have known any differently. Because he came, he blazed a path into progress and culture and civilization. But let the reader beware. No history comes with the bare bones of biography. The bones are usually dripping with the remnants of raw experiences. The sinews of a life cannot be divorced from the dry bones of factual reporting.

There is a purpose here. This story is not just about biography. The story is about history. We will be as faithful to the chronicle as Adriaan's memory and journals allow, and his circle of intimates can piece together. No one tells everything. No one remembers it exactly. The measure of a man is understood by the losses he endures as much as by the accomplishments he realizes. In the end, his story will be interpreted less by the sands of time than by the expanse of eternity.

The scanty work reports and matter-of-fact statements of a Dutch expat do little to tell the story. How to get at the story? Do we look at a slice of life in 1972 that gathered the single largest gathering of Ndugas in one place? It took the mission organization forty flights to gather people from their scattered valleys. Three hundred pigs were slaughtered in a feast for the ages.

Do you measure it in baptisms, or landings and take-offs or pig feasts? In a pig culture, it would be hard to top the Ndugas for sheer extravagance. In a dustup or local skirmish, they were masters of intrigue and bravado.

Or do you tell it in terms of droughts and plagues and accidents and deaths and tribal wars and murders, compiling some type of catalogue to impress and sway the reader by the sheer volume of the case studies amassed as evidence?

Do you measure the results in terms of the trudging or the drudgery, the successes or the setbacks? What makes the case most eloquently for Adriaan van der Bijl's story? Is it in terms of personal suffering, or disappointments and promises unkept that we best convey it?

Could we parade statistics of baptisms and courses taught, students trained, pastors ordained, programs initiated, and conferences hosted to convince and arraign arguments validating Adriaan's achievement?

We could measure it in trips and trails, and clinics and churches, weather delays and airplane parts, and mishaps and misunderstandings. But it is mainly told in God's grace of endurance that measured a man who knew why he had come, and the reason he was there. God's hand was on his life and Adriaan obeyed God's call.

Achievement is not the point. Legacy is not what he is after. It is about the quiet strength of a man who would not quit and who did not complain as the blows of hardship, deprivation, and bereavement assaulted his life. That is the point. By the grace of God, he never quit. He kept on going.

What we can extrapolate from the threads of Adriann's life is perhaps best understood through the eyes of Adriaan's compatriot, Corrie ten Boom, whose image of the threads behind the tapestry of her life, remind us graphically that what you see is not always what you get. There is a perspective that is transcendental, and that adds the shading and colour, and brings the person and his work to life. This book is about the mangled knots and the straggly underbelly of the tapestry. It will be up to the reader to turn the pages, flip the tapestry from time to time, and enjoy the view of the developing picture as it unfolds.

Richard Reichert
Colleague-at-Arms with Adriaan
and the C&MA family

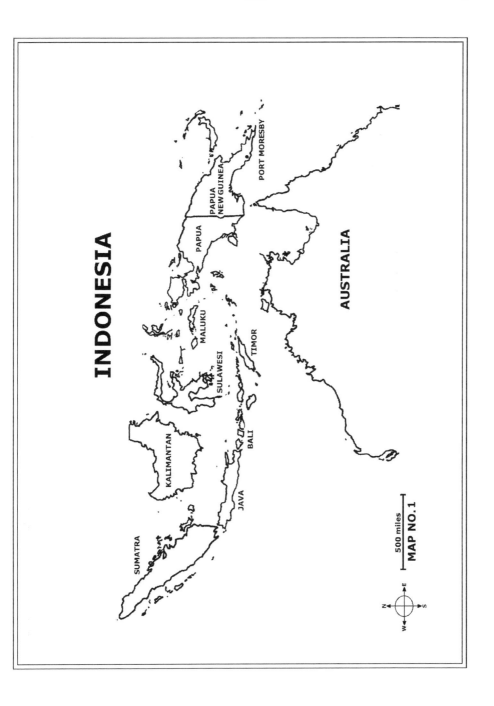

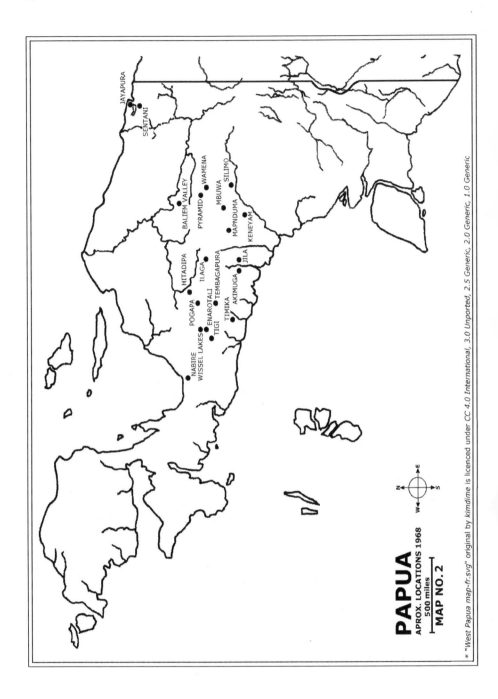

PAPUA

APROX. LOCATIONS 1968

500 miles

MAP NO. 2

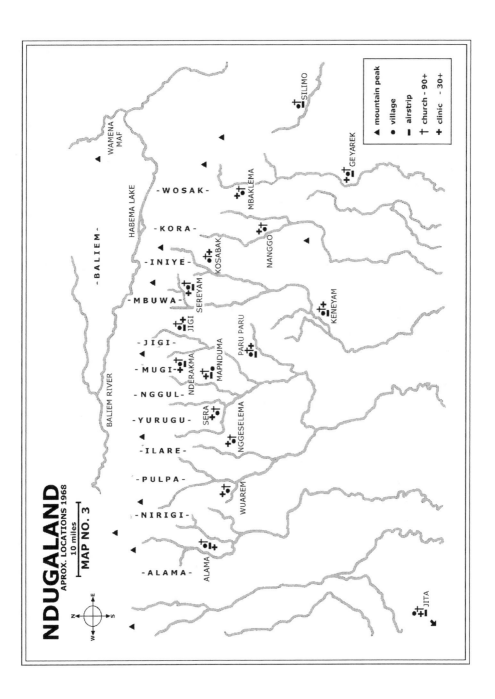

NDUGALAND
APROX. LOCATIONS 1968
10 miles
MAP NO. 3

mountain peak
village
airstrip
† church - 90+
✚ clinic - 30+

SILIMO
GEYAREK
MBAKLEMA
-WOSAK-
-KORA-
KOSABAK
NANGGO
-INIYE-
SEREYAM
-MBUWA-
JIGI
KENEYAM
PARU PARU
-JIGI-
MAPNDUMA
-MUGI-
NDERAKMA
-NGGUL-
SERA
-YURUGU-
NGGESELEMA
-ILARE-
-PULPA-
WUAREM
-NIRIGI-
ALAMA
-ALAMA-
JITA

WAMENA
MAF
HABEMA LAKE
-BALIEM-
BALIEM RIVER

1

MAPNDUMA, A DESTINY

ON THE LIP OF A GORGE, on a precipitous drop-off leading to nowhere, Adriaan van der Bijl bedded down for his first night in a tent in the rain forest. He fell asleep to the sound of crickets, snoring companions, and birds of paradise squawking raucous protests. He dreamt of an audacious venture.

Visions of airstrips, not sugar plums, danced across his mind, as ants and assorted vermin crisscrossed his face and demanded equal billing with the mosquitoes that parachuted through the net. Tropical birdcalls ricocheted through the jungle, waking him up.

Adriaan was no stranger to strange places. Born in Sumatra, educated in Indonesia, Dutch by ancestry, he knew how to steer a dugout canoe before he learned how to skate the rivers of his homeland.

In some ways, it seemed like Adriaan had been heading for Nduga territory all his life.

Putting his pillow down for the first time on the rim of a cliff hugging the edge of the valley was the culmination of years of homing in on his destiny. It seemed like the crosshairs of his compass had been set on Mapnduma and the Nduga people since childhood.

The Nduga people live in the highlands of Papua, the western half of the island of New Guinea. Papua is Indonesia's easterly province. Indonesia, a former Dutch colony, gained independence in 1948, with the exception of Dutch New Guinea, which did not become an Indonesian province until 1963. It has been known under a variety of names, including Dutch New Guinea, West Irian, and Irian Jaya. Today it is the Indonesian province of Papua. Before World War II, little was known about the remote interior of Papua, but during the war, attention was drawn to hundreds of villages in those isolated valleys. Here lived tribes who had been cut off from the rest of the world for centuries. Impenetrable swamps to the north and south of the mountain ranges imprisoned them. There were no roads to the interior, as there are today.

Mapnduma may not be the end of the world, but you can see it from there. Mountainous would be an understatement. Isolated would be a gross understatement.

Papua is the world's second largest island, about ninety miles north of Australia, and about the same distance as the stretch of water between Cuba and the Florida Keys. The western half belongs to Indonesia. It is in this region of the world that Adriaan spent his adult life, trudging the Nduga valleys.

The Ndugas lived in the Stone Age, a primitive highland people who lived in the valleys nestled south of the spine of mountains that run the full length of Papua. They were survivors who worked hard to grow sweet potatoes and a few other vegetables in their gardens on the very steep mountainsides. Stone axes were used to fell trees and split them up, providing material for the fences as well as boards for their thatched huts. Rattan and other jungle vines were used to hold everything together.

They believed spirits must be appeased to evade the harm that controlled their world. They lived in constant fear of the enemy, the evil spirits, and of death.

A Predictable Beginning

Adriaan's first stint in Papua was the most predictable. His father had been an international teacher and administrator in the Dutch-held island of Sumatra, a few dozen large islands and 2,348 miles west of Papua. Adriaan understood education in foreign settings from the ground up. He had been raised in bilingual schools. So, when his mission agency asked him to teach in the Wissel Lakes area of Dutch New Guinea, it was a natural fit. His first assignment as an international mission worker pointed Adriaan in the direction of his final destination.

Within a year, Adriaan was asked to take on expanded responsibility as Superintendent of Schools. Besides teaching, he was given oversight of all government schools in the region. He relished the new job travelling from school to school. He was always up to a new challenge.

But beyond the constant pressure of not being able to fill all the needs for teachers, other winds unsettled Adriaan's spirit. Indonesia wanted the province to be included in their republic. The military began to infiltrate the territory. He was an employee of the Dutch government, and the looming face of independence was sweeping the country. He could see the writing on the wall.

> "We are only four days away from a name change in this country. It will no longer be Dutch New Guinea. The evacuation of all the Dutch is in full swing. We have no idea what will happen in the coming weeks."

Rather than lamenting the end of this era, Adriaan and his wife, Mijo, sent word to the family of their excitement about the future.

"Our work with the schools is almost finished, and we can start in February with normal mission work. That is why we came here."

It was only with time that Adriaan came to understand how strategic his short posting as Superintendent of Schools had been.

A Bundle of Sticks

While Adriaan was evaluating the government school in Hitadipa, a group of Nduga men came to see him with a little bundle of sticks. They put the bundle in his hand, saying, "There are only a few Nduga people in Hitadipa.

Our tribe mostly lives south of the ranges. Would you be their *Bapa*—missionary?" He told them he was in the teaching business and could not accept their request.

When the authorities told the Dutch government to leave Dutch New Guinea, the visit from the Ndugas popped into Adriaan's mind.

> "I still had that little bundle of sticks. Lord, is this what you want me to do? To go to the Nduga tribe south of the ranges very far away from where I now am?"

In the organizational culture of the Christian and Missionary Alliance (C&MA) who had accepted Adriaan to this international posting, protocol and policy had been firmly entrenched by the DNA of its founder. A Presbyterian pastor from Canada, A.B. Simpson had grown disenchanted with the cumbersome structure and lack of interest in missions of the established church. He decided to create an organization that was mobile and military. People signed up for mission work with no assurances that they would ever return. The people who enlisted knew the risks but applied anyway. By the time Adriaan reached Dutch New Guinea, the C&MA had been established for more than sixty years. The fruit of that work had created national church entities in some instances, including the Dutch Alliance Mission that had sent Adriaan to Papua.

The original DNA of the C&MA was still intact—submission to constituted authority and a clear understanding of going where you were assigned and going by established policy when it came to assignments and locations.

It was natural that Adriaan did not pick up his bundle of sticks and head for Nduga country. As a matter of practice, the annual administrative gathering of his Society would decide for him. Repeatedly during his career, where he went was the decision of his peers and leaders under God's guidance who confirmed and appointed him.

Forerunners[1]

The people in the highlands of Papua followed an animistic belief system.

---

[1]Credit for this section is given to Alice Gibbons, author of *The People Time Forgot*. Christian Publications. Camp Hill, Pennsylvania. 1981

They worshiped objects of nature and made appeasement to evil spirits. Animism is characterized by fetishes to ward off evil spirits. It is a religion of fear, fear of evil spirits, fear of the enemy, and fear of death. The tribal people in the highlands of Papua had never heard about God. They did not have a word for God. These animistic people knew something was missing in their lives.

A Damal chief from the Ilaga Valley travelled throughout the mountainous interior looking for what the Damals called *hai*—eternal life. He searched and searched. Before he died, he told his son, Den, "All my life I have searched for eternal life but have not found it. You keep looking. Perhaps in your lifetime, you will find it."

Den never forgot his father's words. The Damal tribe had a legend where the snake and bird raced. They believed that if the snake won the race, they would have hai. They were sad when the bird won. They had lost eternal life. Deep inside their hearts was a vacuum, a God-shaped void that only God could fill. They continued to wait and look for the day when someone would come and show them the way to eternal life.

Then one day Den's son, Sam, told him, "Father, spirit beings have come to the Ilaga Valley. *Tuans*—white men." You can imagine the excitement that rose in Den's heart. God in his sovereignty had put two missionaries together. Those two men were C&MA missionaries Don Gibbons and Gordon Larson. In 1956, Don and Gordon went on a trek to the Ilaga Valley. Don was planning to open a station to reach the Damal tribe and Gordon to reach the Danis.

Sam greeted Don Gibbons in Indonesian. Don was delighted to find an Indonesian speaker whom he could understand. Sam brought a message from his father, Den, who like Sam's grandfather was an important Damal chief. Would Don please come to see him in his village? Don was surprised and went to see him right away. Sam translated as his father spoke, "Greetings and welcome to my village," he began. "I am glad you have come. Let us be friends. You should come and live here with us. I have chosen a site that I will give you to build your house."

The Damals Choose to Follow God

With Sam's help, Don was soon telling Bible stories to the Damals. He began to explain eternal life, talking about Joshua 24:15 where Joshua says, "Choose for yourselves this day whom you will serve." Don told the people that they had a choice. They could follow God or continue to live the way they had always lived. After a lengthy explanation of what it involved, he gave an invitation, "All those who want to follow God, please stand up." All the men rose to their feet. Feeling that they did not understand, Don told them to sit down and went through the details again. When he repeated the invitation, all the men rose again. In disbelief, he told them to be seated and explained everything again. He gave the third invitation, and everyone rose. They said, "We understand what you are saying. We have been waiting for someone to come, and finally, you have brought this message of eternal life to us." Don was overwhelmed. The response to the gospel in Den's village was all-embracing.

One day the Damal men came to Don to say, "We know it is wrong to have our fetishes of spirit worship and our weapons of war used to kill people. What shall we do with them?" Don led them to the book of Acts, where the people burned their magical books. "Oh," they said, "That is what we will do. We will burn them."

Awhile later they invited Don to be present at their fetish burning. "Be careful. There are many non-believing villagers around. If you burn all your bows and arrows, they could kill you," he warned them.

"Don't dissuade us," they said. "We have decided to follow God all the way, and we want you to be there." Don was there. So were the unbelievers and enemies. These people in their superstition thought that when the fetishes were gone, the evil spirits would be angry, and their sweet potatoes would dry up, and the pigs would die. Despite the threats, the believers burned their ancestral fetishes dancing and singing the words: Jesus is more powerful than the evil spirits.

Discipleship Begins

A team of C&MA missionaries began to write the Damal language and teach the people. Don and Alice Gibbons, John and Helen Ellenberger, Mary Owen and Mary Friesen began to disciple them. They started a Witness School teaching a group of twenty men and their wives Bible stories and literacy four days a week and then sent them to the surrounding villages to teach the stories to other people on the weekends. These men became known as Witness Men. During the year, the Damals learned many Bible stories and verses. Matthew 24:14 galvanized them: This gospel of the Kingdom shall be preached in the whole world for a witness to all nations, and then the end shall come. When they realized Jesus would not return until the last tribe heard, they got busy. They wanted to tell everyone about eternal life.

During their summer break from school, the Witness Men sought God's guidance as to where to go to share the good news. Kama Kama, one of the Witness Men, had a God-given burden and passion for reaching the Nduga tribe. He gathered a small group of people together who could speak the Nduga language and set off on a two-week trek over the mountains and through the jungle from his village in the Ilaga Valley. They might be killed, but they and many others were praying and knew God was leading them to share the message of eternal life with the Ndugas.

When the party arrived at Mapnduma, they were no longer afraid. God had prepared the Nduga people through visions and dreams. Something wonderful was coming their way. The Ndugas welcomed Kama Kama who immediately began teaching them about God, creation, sin, and God's Son Jesus Christ who came to give them eternal life. They listened intently with a deep longing for *naberal kaberal*—eternal life. Jesus Christ has the secret of naberal kaberal. Kama Kama had come to share with them who Jesus Christ was. They were overjoyed.

There was so much to learn. The Nduga people did not know that there were seven days in a week. Kama Kama strung up seven cobs of corn and counted them off day by day. When Sunday came along, he explained that Sunday was the day set aside by God to worship and praise the Lord. They were not to gather sweet potatoes in their gardens that day. Every day Kama Kama taught them more Bible stories and verses as they gathered to learn more about this wonderful gospel of good news. He selected promising leaders as elders to teach and guide the Mapnduma people.

When Kama Kama announced that he would be leaving, the men were upset: "How can you do this to us?" Kama Kama told them, "I have taught you all I know; now I must go home and learn more. You need a missionary to put the Bible into your language. Keep praying. God has ears. You will know you are getting a missionary when you see an airplane fly overhead."

The Nduga people waited and waited—hoping, looking, listening for that airplane to fly overhead. The time came when they could wait no longer. They had heard that an airstrip was being built at Jila, near the Ilaga Valley. There was a missionary there. So a group of Nduga men set out for Jila.

C&MA missionaries Frank Ross and John Ellenberger were in Jila overseeing the building of their airstrip. It was tedious and slow going with rocks to dynamite and other obstacles. Weeks had stretched into months. Frank was excited to welcome this party of Nduga men who had come to see him. They gathered each morning to hear the Word of God, which was translated into Nduga for them. They joined in helping to build the airstrip. They worked hard, all the while reciting the new Bible verses they had just learned.

Then one day the Nduga men gathered off by themselves. Frank was curious so went over to find out what they wanted. Their response was, "Would you have another Bible lesson for us at noon?" He was quite surprised at the request and eager to teach them another Bible verse.

It wasn't long before the Ndugas went on strike again. Frank got an interpreter to find out what their issue was this time. It was similar to the first one.

The men told Frank, "We did not come here to earn your earthly possessions, your salt, soap, machetes and steel axes. We came here to learn the Word of God. Could you have another service for us at night?" Frank had never met anyone with such a hunger for God. They enthusiastically gathered for more teaching and helped to complete the airstrip with no more disturbances.

When the airstrip was finished, the Ndugas asked Frank to become their missionary. They were disappointed when he declined and requested that he consider coming on a trek with them to see their area. Frank knew how jagged and steep the mountainous terrain was, but God urged him to go.

In every village, the Nduga people begged Frank for a missionary to teach them the Word of God.

2

THE ARRIVAL

UNKNOWN TO THE NDUGAS, God had their missionary picked out for them. Adriaan van der Bijl had received his marching orders from the C&MA leadership and was preparing for the momentous opportunity. It was at the July 1963 C&MA Annual Conference that a team of four, Adriaan and Mijo van der Bijl, Mary Owen, and Elfrieda Toews, were assigned to start a work with the Nduga tribe. It was time to bundle up the sticks and move on.

"We do not know a lot about the Ndugas. We understand that the people have waited a long time and that some people have already burned their fetishes and are waiting for someone to teach them more about the Jesus way.

It seems that this tribe is very open-hearted and helpful. The Nduga character has impressed many missionaries. Some say whoever gets this tribe will get the best. We are looking forward to meeting them and doing our best to teach them."

When You Hear a Plane

An aerial survey was the first step. As Adriaan flew over Nduga territory, he saw a few places that would be suitable for an airstrip. Mbuwa, Iniye, and Mapnduma were possible sites. God directed Adriaan to choose Mapnduma as the place to build an airstrip and settle.

"When the Ndugas heard the plane overhead, they were excited. "We are going to get our Bapa! Where shall we go to meet him? We might as well go to Jila. Maybe he will land there." Since they had connected with Frank Ross at Jila when they helped him build the airstrip, they decided to go back to Jila. They headed off."

Meanwhile, Adriaan prepared for the two-week trek to Mapnduma to determine where to place an airstrip. Besides a tent and foodstuffs, he needed a radio, a little battery-powered box with an antenna and handset, vital for communications.

The day before he was to fly into Jila to begin the trek, Frank called him on the radio to say, "I don't know how we can have enough people to carry your stuff. Our people here are not interested in going." Adriaan wondered where they would get the carriers they needed. He would be trekking with Frank Ross and Harold Catto, the Field Chairman. It would not be an easy trip, but the flight to Jila was arranged. He committed it to the Lord to work it out.

That was the day the group of Nduga men came out of the jungle at Jila. They found Frank Ross to ask, "Where is our Bapa? We heard and saw that little airplane coming around." Startled at their arrival and question, Frank recovered enough to reply, "He is coming tomorrow."

"I arrived the next day to learn that the Nduga men arrived at the
precise time we needed them. It was an amazing provision from
the Lord as he promised in Isaiah 65:24 that before they call, he
will answer and while they are yet speaking, he will hear."

The next morning the mountain was obscured by a fog that clung to the valley, stubborn and uninviting. The trail that beckoned was tortuous, winding
up and down the rugged mountains, passing village after village.

"At thirty-three years of age, I was ready for the challenge. The
Nduga carriers were loaded down with aluminum containers that
contained food for the two-week trek to Mapnduma. They were
happy to carry my stuff—a tent, the two-way shortwave radio
and battery, shovels, axes and machetes to build the airstrip. An
Nduga man, who knew Indonesia, served as our interpreter."

At each village, the people welcomed them. Each evening, they set up camp,
started a little fire to cook their food, and pitched their tent for the night.
While the Ndugas ate their sweet potato staple, Adriaan prepared canned
meat, beans or tomatoes with freshly cooked rice. Some Ndugas were surprised to discover there was other meat in the world besides pork.

It was a journey into a world filled with shades of green with the moss-
es adding their distinctive bright hues. The trail that led them through the
often-impenetrable rainforest was steep and slippery, and often they hung
onto protruding vines to keep from sliding. Many times, a slick pole bridge

with notches slashed into it helped them across a rushing stream on all fours. At other times, the Ndugas cut down trees, carrying them down the mountain and laying them over the torrents for a makeshift bridge.

They had the adventure of sitting in a hoop sliding along a large forest vine that was suspended from one side of the river to the other to get across the raging waters below.

"On October 31, 1963 we came to the top of the last mountain which brought Mapnduma into view. Suddenly the carriers stopped and began to hoot and shout and dance. We saw the people in Mapnduma running in circles dancing, shouting and hooting in response. Our hearts began to pound with excitement.

Our entire party joined them, dancing and singing with delight. We had arrived! The people were so happy to see us. They had waited so long to have their own Bapa. I received a grandiose welcome like none other. It was a day I will never forget.

Some people had been exposed to the message of Christ when Kama Kama had visited earlier. Nduga evangelists, trained in the Moni Bible School at Hitadipa by Bill and Gracie Cutts, had also taught and instructed them in the Word of God. The Ndugas had already prepared a shelter of upright poles in the ground covered with grass for church services in preparation for my coming as their resident missionary."

While on the trail, Adriaan had used the two-way radio as little as possible to conserve battery life. When a Mission Aviation Fellowship (MAF) plane dropped a generator and fuel, Adriaan was finally in full contact with the outside world.

"The next day, November 1, 1963 I was in contact with MAF by radio, asking that they bring in supplies. They flew over and dropped more tools, shovels, and axes needed to construct the airstrip."

Five Weeks to Landing and Take Off

Adriaan, with Dutch Reformed roots, had already travelled light years in the direction of a more charismatic view of the universe. He knew the God who can talk to us and usually does if we care to listen. As the airstrip project began, Adriaan admits he had been getting indications from higher up. As he glanced at one of the Nduga wooden fences, he saw the shape of the number five outlined in the configuration of the fencing. Immediately, he felt the assurance that this was a sign from God. He thought to himself, "The airstrip will take five weeks, five months, or five years to complete." It gave him the motivation to work hard to have it ready for landing in five weeks.

If the lifeline of radio communication was essential gear for the missionary, the airstrip would become its life blood. It was where visitors arrived, officials were received, where children came and left. Births and deaths, evacuations and send-offs would all flow out from the little ribbon of grass on the lip of the mountain.

Life in Mapnduma would be measured by landings and airdrops. It would be gauged by load weights and passenger lists registered in log books. The airstrip would be the communications hub of the settlement, a place where people wept and laughed, mourned and celebrated. Cargo and passengers, medicine, building supplies, tools, fuel and food, cows and chickens, everything from calendars to sheets of aluminum came by air.

First, the airstrip must be built. Someone must pay the price. This Adriaan understood. There were dark dramas ahead that not even Adriaan could imagine. For now, he knew that God was telling him to build the airstrip.

"God has assured me that this airstrip would be completed in five weeks. That was a human impossibility. Airstrips always took quite awhile to build. Frank Ross, along with John Ellenberger, had worked on the Jila airstrip for a year. Once an airstrip was finished, MAF personnel had to come in to inspect it for safety before they would allow their planes to use it.

On the first day, 200-300 excited Ndugas gathered to start clearing heavy trees and dense underbrush chanting: Let's work. Let's work. Let nobody shirk. They were so eager to get started that they dug with their sticks and poles until the proper tools arrived."

Soon tools were falling from the sky via the MAF drops. Mijo came along on one drop. As the plane circled for her to push out the load, she caught sight of her beloved Adriaan. Instead of pushing it out, she waved and waved. The pilot had to circle three times before she finally pushed the things out the door.

"After a faith-filled devotional and prayer each morning, hundreds of people worked on the airstrip. The work moved ahead quickly. In exactly five weeks, on December 5, 1963 at five p.m. we finished the airstrip just as the Lord had promised me!

Because Mapnduma was so far out of the way, MAF decided to entrust me with the responsibility to prepare and then check the airstrip properly. They gave me strict instructions to follow. That next week, the first landing was made without MAF walking in to inspect it first.

Mijo and our three children, Daniel, age 3, David, 17 months old, and Heidi, 3 months flew in on the second flight to begin their time at Mapnduma living in a tent and enjoying the wonderful friendliness of the Nduga people. Just before Christmas we moved into our little house."

Mary Owen and Elfrieda Toews got their first look at their future home when they arrived for the dedication of the airstrip on January 17, 1964. Pilot Clell Rogers, representing MAF, stayed for the service. Frank Ross, who had been instrumental in opening the work with the Ndugas, delivered the message. People trekked in from around the area with hooting, shouting, singing and dancing, a celebration of praise to God for answering years of prayer.

During the prayer of dedication, men representing each valley in Ndugaland stood together, hand-in-hand, to consecrate the airstrip. Having representatives from each valley involved in the dedication was important to show everyone present that the Ndugas, although from numerous valleys and dialects, were of one accord.

The airstrip was completely cleaned up and all debris hauled away by the beginning of February. The men who helped construct it were paid and happily headed back to their valleys, mission accomplished!

Their Bapa had arrived!

The Ndugas were no longer saying they were the last cucumber on the vine. No longer were they without a Bapa. No longer were they left hanging while other tribes were learning about eternal life. The vine was flourishing and showing signs of sprouting more shoots. It was the beginning of the realization that the Nduga jungle paradise would produce abundant fruit for the Kingdom of God.

3

THE GATHERING STORM

ADRIAAN'S STORY BEGAN SOME YEARS BEFORE, on the island of Sumatra, 2400 miles west of Papua. The fourth child of Adriaan and Sijtje Anna Margaretha van der Bijl, he was born on November 19, 1929 in the same house as three older siblings, Egbert, Jan Willem, and Wilhelmina, in Narumonda, Sumatra, Indonesia.

His father worked as a teacher in a Dutch-run school under the Rheinish Mission. He taught the Batak children the Dutch language as well as Indonesian along with their other subjects.

Because they were missionary children, Adriaan and his siblings attended church every Sunday. Adriaan was baptized as a little child in the Christian Reformed Church.

Life in Narumonda, Sumatra was wonderful. Until Adriaan was old enough to attend school, he was free to explore his world and play with the children that lived around him. He learned to speak their local dialect, Batak.

When Adriaan was five years old, his family moved to Sigompoelon just outside of Tarutung. They were hardly settled into their new home when a new adventure began. He had heard of furlough and Holland. Now he got to find out what this was all about.

Front row: Nel, Sijtje with Frieda, Liesbeth, Adriaan Sr., Adriaan
Back row: Jan Willem, Wilhelmina, Egbert

By this time, his family consisted of twelve-year-old Egbert, ten-year-old Jan Willem, seven-year-old Willhelmina, plus Adriaan at five years of age, nearly four-year-old Liesbeth and two-year-old Nel. They travelled to Holland where they lived with Uncle Gerard and Aunt Rietje Schaap until his father found a house in Alphen aan de Rijn, near the Rhine River. The children went to school while Adriaan's father and mother visited with family and rested.

This was the first time that Adriaan had been away from the tropical climate. When winter came, he found Holland desperately cold and unpleasant. Ice skating on the river was one way to pass the time after school was over, but he couldn't wait to get back to year-round warmth in Indonesia.

They lived on the school campus where Adriaan's father was Headmaster of over 500-600 Indonesian students. He had two Dutch teachers who likely had Indonesian teaching assistants. Each classroom had a teacher responsible for teaching three grades.

Adriaan's family enjoyed music. They played records on the gramophone and gathered around the organ to sing hymns and psalms. Father and mother both played the organ, something the children did not learn.

When Adriaan was six years old, he attended the school for Dutch children in the nearby village of Tarutung. He loved the trail that they walked every morning going up and over the mountain slope to the school. When school was over each afternoon, they would retrace their steps back home. One day a surprise awaited him, baby Frieda had joined their family.

Their school was taught in the Dutch language and carried the Dutch cultural emphasis, with the Queen's picture and the Dutch flag in prominent places. A special holiday was Koninginnedag—Queen's Day—on April 30. The National anthem, Het Wilhelmus, was sure to be sung on this day.

The class was likely between thirty to forty children. They were taught in Dutch with cultural and religious training mixed in with all the academics that were required.

Adriaan went through to grade six during the time he attended there. As he advanced through the grades, he found that math was a subject that interested him almost as much as recess. During recess, there was time for a few rounds of marbles or maybe a game of soccer or volleyball.

After they finished their education at Tarutung, Adriaan's brother, Jan Willem and sister, Wilhelmina, had to go to the Planter's School. This large boarding school at Brastagi was provided for the Dutch children.

Adriaan had lived the carefree and protected life of expat children of Dutch missionaries to Sumatra for his first eleven years. He was more at home in Indonesia than in his home culture. He spoke Batak and had Indonesian friends but lived the sheltered, if not pampered, life of a child of foreigners.

Something of the prestige of the mission-led schools gives clues into how much an education in foreign-led schools was prized and how much Adriaan's father was revered by the Batak students. This becomes part of the thread of Adriaan's life when he becomes a Superintendent of Schools.

Adriaan's photo albums show pictures of him living in Tarutung in 1937 when eight years old. Those childhood days were not to last forever. All too soon they were rudely interrupted by war. Boyhood pranks, lazy days of exploring, girlfriends and exquisite family vacations came crashing down around Adriaan when the Japanese invaded Sumatra. His oldest brother had returned to Holland in 1938 to further his education, but in May 1940 the letters stopped. Germany had invaded the Netherlands. Years later, they learned that their uncle was involved with the underground movement, protecting the Jews from the Germans. One day the authorities came to the house and arrested Adriaan's uncle as well as Egbert. They were taken to a prison camp in Germany.

World War II touched everyone including Adriaan. Suddenly, the Germans Adriaan had so happily played with, were now the enemy. They were rounded up and put in camps with barricades until they could be removed from the country. It was sad for the children, heartbreaking for their parents. The Japanese slowly moved all over Asia, through China, the Philippines, and finally, the Dutch East Indies, invading Sumatra via Singapore. They started in Medan and slowly gathered all the Dutch people into different camps.

"My father, now forty-four years old, was called up for military service by the Dutch government, who controlled Sumatra, to protect the island against the Japanese invasion. The call to service was too little, too late. Father was soon captured and imprisoned by the enemy forces.

We heard on the radio that the Japanese were slowly coming our way. The Dutch leadership told my mother to move into

Tarutung so we could be close to the rest of the people. We hurriedly packed a few clothes and blankets together. We didn't even pack food. My brother Jan Willem grabbed the silverware. He headed outside, dug a hole and buried it in the yard."

Even in the confusion and danger a boy's mind is at work. The Dutch army had some fuel tanks near their home. To prevent the Japanese from benefiting from the fuel, the army decided to blow up the tanks. Adriaan and his friends decided they could see the explosion of the fuel tanks much better if they were higher up.

"We climbed higher on the mountainside. From there, we had a safe and spectacular view as the fuel tanks exploded. When it was safe, we checked the mission compound. It had not been harmed in the explosion. We were able to move back into the house. We continued to hear the reports about the Japanese advance by radio. I was very upset.

The next day, March 15, 1942, the Japanese arrived. They looked so unthreatening as they pedalled into view on their bicycles. When they started shouting and waving their weapons, we began to pay attention. All the Dutch were rounded up and herded into Tarutung. The soldiers could not speak either Dutch or Indonesian, but made their commands clear as they shouted and gestured.

I can still see the Japanese soldiers coming up to our house commanding us to move out of it. The small Dutch community of about fifty or sixty people was all herded into Teeken's house. As night came on, we realized that we would have to sleep on the floor. We huddled together behind closed doors. The house felt so small and crowded.

Then Japanese soldiers started banging on the door, demanding that the single ladies be sent out so that they could have their way with them. The Dutch men refused, blocking their entrance."

The next day they were moved to the Governor's residence. The women and children were ordered to the campus in Sigompoelon and on April 11, after three and a half weeks at the boarding school, the men were sent to Pearadja, the village next to Sigompoelon.

On May 6, the men were herded into trucks. They travelled for some hours and were ordered out when they arrived at Pematang Siantar, where the Japanese gathered together all the Dutch people from northern Sumatra. They were in that location for almost a year. The heat was oppressive, night and day.

> "There was so much confusion in the beginning. Once the men were separated from the women and children in different camps, there was to be no communication between the two groups. Father was able to get little messages to Mother from time to time."

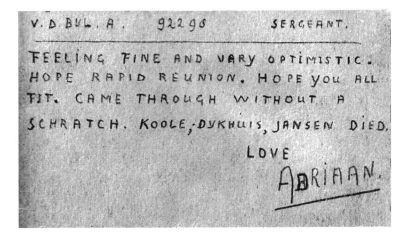

On December 21, they were moved again, to a mountain town, Brastagi, which was much cooler, a more pleasant temperature. This had been the Planter's School where Adriaan's brother and sister had studied before the war started. There were now about 1,800 women and children there.

> "The Japanese had not brought our mattresses with us, so we slept on the hard floor for several nights. When the mattresses did arrive, most of them were wet and forty had to be burned because of lice infestations."

Now the food was less plentiful. About 1,000 people could eat in the dining room, and the other 800 had to pick up their food in pails. The menu consisted of corn porridge and one piece of bread for breakfast, a lunch of rice, meat and veggies, and one fruit, and an evening meal of soup and two pieces of bread.

"Time dragged on. We were isolated and only got fragments of news from time to time. Christmas came. My mother and the other women tried to make the day special. A big Christmas tree was set up in the dining room. In the afternoon, they organized a celebration and an evening service with a girls' choir.

Our family was scattered that Christmas. Father was in the military prison, Egbert in Holland, Jan Willem in the men's prison in Siantar. The rest of us in Brastagi felt very lonely without them."

On February 14, 1943, an important visitor came to the camp. It was announced that the older boys in the camp were to go to the men's camp at Soegei Sengkol. The boys were asked to volunteer if they were willing to go. Adriaan volunteered. Four days later, they were moved to the men's camp, close to Medan, but quite far from his mother and sisters.

His brother, Jan Willem, was already at that camp. Everyone had his own bed and was able to wear his own clothes. Bedbugs and lice abounded. Most chose to go barefoot as their shoes wore out. Organized classes were set up, although learning became more difficult as they got hungrier. Drinking water came from wells, but bathing had to be done in the river.

"We were only allowed out of the camp to bathe. The rules were that we were not to go into the dam. One time some of us decided to go swimming in it despite the rules. We were all naked as we enjoyed the freedom of a good swim.

Then the Japanese saw us!

A guard ordered us out of the water and slapped us across the face, something I had never experienced before. We were not allowed to go out there anymore. If anybody dared to crawl under or over the barbwire fence to get food, they were severely beaten."

Then the Japanese built a very primitive camp at the end of the railroad, 125-185 miles from the men's camp.

> "I think they planned to get rid of all of us. We were shipped by train to Sirengo Rengo. The ten rattan bamboo barracks held 200-300 people. We had to sleep on wooden platforms built one above another. I slept on the top, which was about six feet above the floor. Each man got about 30 inches of space, to store our personal stuff. We used mosquito nets to protect us. Bed bugs and ants were everywhere."

Bathroom facilities were non-existent. For the first while, they used the river. Later, they dug a deep trench called the trem. There was no toilet paper. The hygiene situation was horrible.

> "Because the outhouses were quite far away, someone with dysentery just squatted outside to relieve himself. When it rained, the area was one big mud pool. People became very thin and were unable to work in the gardens. We had to get the wood out of the jungle and it had to be carried into the camp as fuel for cooking. The river was where we bathed, if the guards and the crocodiles permitted it. It was difficult for older men.
>
> We had to line up for gruel, which was cooked in barrels. I was part of the kitchen help, so I could scrape the pots and was able to get a little extra food. We got rice once a day."

Someone must have had a little radio, because war news began to leak out. The Americans had gotten involved after Pearl Harbor. News reached them that Japan had been bombed. The word was that the Japanese did not want any more war.

> "We could see it in the Japanese behavior. Instead of rough and hard people, they became friendly, asking what they could do for us."

Food became available. About 2,000 coconuts were dropped close to the river and brought to the camp. Rice and sweet potato was supplied, and some men insisted that they get tobacco. Adriaan was able to visit the women's camp since the women had been moved to a closer camp. He travelled by train to visit them, and his mother remarked at how fat he was.

> "By then, Mother had heard more information about Father. He had worked, along with the others, to build a railroad into the interior. With so little food, he became sick. By January 1945, Father was very sick with dysentery. He told a friend, Wout van Eck, about a dream he had where he saw a white boat and Egbert was standing on it, waving to him. Shortly after, on January 6, Father died. He didn't know that his son had already died in Germany's Neuengamme Concentration Camp."

He was buried in the camp graveyard. His body was later exhumed and reburied in Java in a big military cemetery.

Early in August 1945, Adriaan's mother and other leaders were called to the camp office. The commander did not say anything about the capitulation but said that a lot of rice and oil was going to be brought into the camp and that everybody could take as much as they wanted. When his mother came back in the barracks, she shouted, "Either the Japs are going crazy or the war is over!"

> "I remember the day that a big airplane flew overhead and dropped all kinds of food. We rejoiced and praised the Lord. On August 24, 1945, we raised the Dutch flag again. The kids pulled down the barricades. They brought in water buffalo for fresh meat. Everyone was giddy with happiness. I was now almost sixteen.
>
> We were not able to leave the area right away as things had to be organized. Eventually we were brought back to Medan and started a life of freedom again. We had our meals at a community kitchen.
>
> Finally, after a year of waiting, we were put on a ship and sailed to Holland. We were welcomed by our family and were taken into various homes until we could locate a home of our own. We moved, together with some other families from Indonesia, into a house in Bloemendaal, not too far from Haarlem.

Mother managed quite well after the war and received a pension from the Dutch government because her husband had died in the service. Introverted and quiet, she was a good cook and provided a peaceful stable life for us."

The war chapter was over, with its pain and loss. It was now time for Adriaan to move forward to his own destiny. He had no idea what that would be, or that it might involve a French girl from southern France. And he had no idea how far that destiny would lead him.

4

A FRENCH GIRL

ADRIAAN MOVED FORWARD with what he imagined would be his lot in life. His dad had been a teacher, so he took three years of teacher training. After mandatory one-year military training with the Royal Netherlands Army, he began his teaching career in Pijnacker, a small town not very far from Den Haag. He was teaching students who finished sixth grade and did not want to go on to higher education.

The threads of the tapestry of Adriaan's life were strongly intertwined with the teaching profession. He was at home in the classroom, and his father's influence was soon apparent in Adriaan's love of teaching.

The Missing Link

It was while teaching school that Adriaan was introduced to a missing thread in the tapestry of his spiritual formation. He connected with a Christian group from America, called the Navigators.

When Adriaan met the Navigator leader, Dan Piatt, he was attracted to his warm and friendly manner.

"I admired the joy and peace that he displayed. He also seemed to be very close to God. I was attracted to this group of people who seemed to think that being Christian was more than being good. They talked as if they knew God personally and they seemed to find the Bible interesting. Their joy and contentment in life was compelling."

Adriaan teaches in Pijnacker, Holland

Adriaan with Dan Piatt

Dan and Adriaan met from time to time either in the Navigator office or at a local coffee shop. Late in 1954, Dan asked him,

"Do you know the Lord?"

"Of course. I go to church every Sunday; besides, my parents were missionaries..."

"No. I don't mean that. Do you know him personally? Have you received him in your heart?"

"Not that I know of. I was baptized..."

Dan then explained to Adriaan what it meant to be a born-again Christian.

"Finally, I understood that I needed to make a personal response to Christ's offer of salvation. Dan guided me as I asked Jesus to be my personal Saviour. A great peace filled me."

The Bible became a book that he wanted to read. Dan taught him how to develop the relationship he now had with Christ.

"I found a great desire growing in me to serve the Lord, possibly with the Navigators somewhere in Europe."

One day Dan asked, "Wouldn't you like to be in the service of the Lord with your missionary background?"

It captivated Adriaan's imagination. He had just been teaching kids in school. Was that all there was for him? This idea struck a chord with a missionary kid, perhaps yearning for something of the cultural magic that had been missing in his life.

"If you want to be in the Lord's service, you will need to get some training in Bible School," Dan advised. He put Adriaan in contact with the European Bible Institute in Chateau, a village close to Paris. It was a small school with thirty students, begun in 1952. Adriaan resigned his teaching position and headed for the Bible Institute.

Most European Bible Institute activities were held in the three-story building. Classrooms, chapel and dining room on the first floor. Ladies on the second floor; men on the third. The chilly men's residence was nicknamed "The North Pole."

Paris in the Spring

When he started classes in the fall of 1955, he had to choose whether to take the courses in English or French. Since he was better in English, he chose that language.

While there, a whole new world opened up for Adriaan. Raised in the staid comfort zone of the Reformed Church world, he was fascinated by the new evangelical world that opened to him.

The music was lively. The students dug into the Word with appetite and shared the truth of God's love openly with others. They developed lifelong friendships and spent their vacations on evangelistic teams that ministered in tent campaigns all through Europe.

And despite the restrictions on opposite sex contact, there were girls. The romantic side of Adriaan found fertile soil in the Paris Bible School setting.

> "One of my classmates, during the three years at the European Bible Institute, was a French girl, Marie Josephe Montet Sperat. Her mother gave her the nickname Mijo by combining parts of her first two names, Marie Josephe. The name stuck."

Adriaan took notice that Mijo was a very spiritual girl who knew God's Word, loved the Lord, and wanted to obey him. When he became aware that she had a boyfriend, he was disappointed, but thought, "The Lord knows what's best for me and I can leave it with him."

> "At the beginning of 1958, I started to pray for her again. It didn't make sense logically. I did not want a foreign girl, much less a French one, because of the language barriers. As I prayed, I asked God to do something impossible. This impossible became possible because she broke off with her boyfriend.
>
> Three months before graduation, I asked her to go for a walk by the Seine River. Using my broken French, I proposed to her. It was a total surprise to her. As we continued our stroll along the riverbank, one of the teachers saw us walking together. We were afraid that we would be expelled from school."

Since they had been seen breaking the rules of the Institute, Adriaan went to

Dr. Barnes, the Director, as soon as they got back to the school and explained the situation to him.

> "He said if we kept our relationship to ourselves until the end of the year, he would not expel us from school.
>
> I did not see Mijo for several days. She was dealing with the question I had asked her. As she prayed for direction, God gave her peace. She agreed to become my wife."

There were several months of quiet love, sitting together in class and eating together in the dining room. At the end of the year, they surprised everybody when they announced their love for each other. Many people, including his mentor, Dan Piatt, thought that Mijo was not the best choice for Adriaan.

They finished their course at the European Bible Institute on June 10, 1958, and let family and friends know that they planned to get married.

> "We went to the southern part of France, where I met Mijo's mother, Madam Sperat. My conversational French was somewhat limited, so Mijo translated for us during our visit. Because Mijo's parents had divorced before this, I never did meet her dad.
>
> I also took Mijo to meet my mother. Since Mother did not speak French, it was a frustrating conversation as we translated our conversation to each other. In spite of the language difficulties, Mother accepted Mijo with a loving, motherly embrace."

An Unexpected Turn

During the summer of 1958, Adriaan travelled for the Navigator's campaigns in Holland, Paris and Germany, where he spent time training youth in camps. He went to the south of France to visit with Mijo, where she had been doing children's work. By the beginning of September, he had settled into the Navigator's headquarters in The Hague.

> "We decided that Mijo should move to Holland to learn the Dutch language and way of life. A family who needed a nanny lived within walking distance of the Navigator's headquarters where I was

living. They hired Mijo. I continued to travel throughout Europe
in my work for the Navigators, believing that this was my calling."

Their wedding date remained up in the air. They prayed for a miracle.
They looked forward to ministry together but the uncertainty of the future
was difficult. They often thought of giving up in frustration.

"The Lord started to talk to me about missions. With my background as a missionary kid in Indonesia, I began to long to return.
But where could I fit in? Indonesia was now independent, with
only New Guinea still under Dutch rule."

One day Adriaan received a pamphlet through the mail. The C&MA needed
teachers in New Guinea immediately. It seemed that this was God's direction. They got in contact with headquarters and were accepted as missionary
teachers. This gave them the freedom to marry on September 23, 1959.

"On the day of our wedding, we received a letter from the C&MA leadership saying that, after our wedding and honeymoon, we could move into the C&MA mission center during the training period. This was one of God's strong confirmations that we were moving forward in step with his purpose. What a wedding gift!

Our honeymoon was on Texel Island. After travelling by train and boat, we spent a week together enjoying the beach and hotel. After our honeymoon, we settled into Parousia, the beautiful villa in Wassenaar owned by the C&MA. Several couples lived in the villa. We studied Indonesian and familiarized ourselves with the vision and doctrinal positions of the C&MA. Then in April 1960 a letter arrived from the New York headquarters: I am happy to inform you that during the April 5-7 meeting of the Board of Managers of the C&MA, you were appointed as missionaries of our society for service in New Guinea. This appointment is in view of your sailing in the summer or early fall of 1960."

Moving in Step with a Divine Calling

On Ascension Sunday, May 15, 1960 a missionary service was held in Rotterdam, with about 800 people present. During the service, Mijo and Adriaan were dedicated to missionary service.

The summer was a whirlwind of activity as they prepared to leave for Dutch New Guinea. They needed to prepare a prayer card, set up speaking engagements to introduce themselves and encourage people to begin to support them in prayer and through finances. By then they were aware that their first child was on the way. Because Mijo was pregnant, the C&MA made the arrangements for them to travel to Dutch New Guinea by air. Instead of several weeks, it took them about three days to get to their destination.

It was one more confirmation that they were moving in step with a divine calling. The road forward would not be easy. Bridges were to be crossed but Adriaan was familiar with bridges. For now all he knew was that he was going home.

5

KINGDOM BUSINESS

THE COST OF DOING KINGDOM BUSINESS in Papua was high. You could measure it in cross-cultural stress levels that are off the charts. You could measure it in the decibels of a tribal war cry piercing the darkness. You could measure it in the sobbing of a mother burying her newborn, or a husband and children burying a mother.

You could measure it in the racing heartbeat of parents applying their braking mechanisms to aid the heart-stopping landing on a grass airstrip with their children on board. Or you could measure the cost of doing Kingdom business in Papua by a mother crying herself to sleep because her children are in boarding school and her husband is over the mountain settling a local tribal squabble.

Or you could measure it by the times the plane could not land because of the weather and people died because medications did not arrive in time. You could measure it by the times the Nduga mother did not take medicine but relied on ancient spirits and dubious potions and poisonous concoctions.

Then you could measure it by the cost in young people reverting to old habits or in elders disappointingly returning to perverse traditions. These and a hundred more reasons would sum the calculation to astronomical figures.

The bottom line is that living in Mapnduma was not for the faint of heart or the weekend adventure crowd. You came because you were driven by a compulsion that reduced the risks. Worrying about the weather passed into oblivion on the spectrum of other provocations from the elements and the culture, the heat and the mildew, the pests and the pestilence that assaulted daily existence.

The first term in Mapnduma for the team of four was the honeymoon stage of establishing a base of operations and building rapport with the Nduga people. Whoever said that the people appointed to the Nduga tribe would be getting the best, was right. The Nduga people were so excited to get their very own missionaries.

Introduction to Mapnduma

Adriaan, Mijo, and their three young children were already there, adjusting to their new home and Nduga life. Language study was a priority. Adriaan had a head start, having learned Indonesian in his early years. Mijo, as well, was bilingual. Mary had spent some years working with the Damal tribe and knew their language. Elfrieda joined her in Ilaga for a few months so they could study the Nduga language together. It would be August 1964 before Elfrieda and Mary would settle in to live among the Nduga population.

Simon Uburuangge, nicknamed Smiley for his contagious smile, was one of the first to welcome the team to Mapnduma. Smiley was in the group who trekked with Adriaan, Frank Ross, and Harold Catto from Jila to Mapnduma to scout out the land and to help select the right spot for the airstrip. He became a pivotal leader in Ndugaland. A District Superintendent for some years, he mentored pastors and spoke out strongly against the demonic false cults as they surfaced.

Smiley had been a war chief, leading his tribe culturally. In danger from warring enemies, he decided to move to another valley. Gathering up his few earthly belongings, he set out over the rugged mountains and across rushing rivers with his wife and young son. They came to Kababo, a village south of Mapnduma. His knees were infected badly, and he had to resort to two walking canes. Hobbling into the village in pain, two Nduga Witness Men from Hitadipa offered to pray for his healing. He had never heard of God. He did not know what prayer was. He declined, saying that he wanted to stick with spirit worship.

The next day, he hovered near the spot where a woman was experiencing a difficult birth. He observed the Witness Men praying for her. The baby was born instantly. Her ordeal was not yet over. The placenta did not deliver. Again, the Witness Men prayed. The placenta slipped out.

Smiley could not believe the instantaneous results. When the Witness Men again offered to pray for him, he gave them permission. That night he went to sleep easily and woke up at midnight to discover that he could move his knees without pain. He jumped up, ran into the courtyard, shouting, "I'm healed. God healed me. No more pain."

From that time on, he never wavered in following the Lord, though persecuted for his faith. God protected him at every turn. He was eager to know more about this new way of life. He absorbed all he could about the God who had healed him. He became a follower of Christ, a servant to all.

Elfrieda met him for the first time at the airstrip dedication in January 1964. From then on, he was involved in every aspect of her life. He guided Elfrieda and Mary to the right spot for their house. He helped the team when they struggled with the language, becoming their interpreter when it was difficult for them to communicate. He was the first to graduate from the Mapnduma Witness School and in the first graduating class of the Sion Bible College.

Smiley became Elfrieda's self-appointed medical assistant. Nearly every afternoon, he arrived about 5:30 p.m to accompany her on her village rounds to visit the sick or dying. When there was an emergency, Smiley was at the door to help Elfrieda walk on sidewalks made with logs, maneuver slippery bridges and mud puddles, leading her to the right hut to treat the patient.

Smiley's first impulse was prayer. Immediately he would lay hands on the patient, calling on the God who healed him to have mercy. He believed in God's touch. With the little grasp of Nduga Elfrieda knew at the time, he would help her decipher the problem so that she could treat appropriately.

In January 1965 when the first Mapnduma Witness School began, Smiley was one of the first to enroll. He studied hard and learned to read and write Nduga so he could lead teams out to the surrounding villages to teach the people there. Courses in the Life of Christ, Old Testament, and Scripture Memorization were taught. To motivate people who never had to be disciplined in their time schedule to go to school regularly was a big accomplishment.

The Witness Men and their wives met every morning from 7:30 until noon. The wives listened from the back of the room while caring for their children. Then they headed off to their gardens to gather sweet potatoes. In the evening the men came, ten at a time, to one of the missionary homes to review the lessons to teach out in the villages on the weekends.

Health Detours

In the attempt to chronicle the van der Bijl story, we can only catalogue the health situations that could have ended their careers: malaria, thyroid, tuberculosis, cancer, pneumonia and hepatitis. Mijo's medical history sounds like a hospital caseload report, not the health report of one person.

We could catalogue the near misses in Mijo's life. Or we could record the direct hits of demonic incursions. It would be impossible to register the log of drudgery and depression masquerading as disappointment that seeped into their spirits at times when common sense said to quit, but they were too spent to recognize it or too weak to care.

Mijo knew the risks. Mijo traded in miracles like some people trade cars. Setbacks and hurdles there would be. The story of how Mijo got there is not as amazing as the fact that she stayed. The bottom line is that Mijo loved God and she loved the Nduga people. Mapnduma was her home. Mijo had come to stay.

As the team was beginning to feel settled into Mapnduma life, the first signs of something wrong appeared. Instead of setting up her home and interacting with the people, Mijo and Adriaan were flying to Port Moresby, the capital of Papua New Guinea, for surgery. Her thyroid was acting up. To get there from Mapnduma they had to fly to Sentani near Jayapura, Indonesia and back across the expanse of Papua New Guinea to Port Moresby.

The surgery went well, but there were complications.

> "Within twenty-four hours after Mijo's surgery on November 4, 1966, she began to feel unwell. By evening, she could hardly breathe and was feeling cold and numb. The doctors came just in time and did an emergency operation on the spot. The surgery site was hemorrhaging. When they stopped the bleeding, the symptoms stopped. However, the healing process had to start all over again. Right after that, she started running a high fever. The doctor speculated that she was having another bout of malaria."

She did not return to Mapnduma for five months. The usually stoic Adriaan could not disguise his disappointment.

> "This will be a year to remember. It was not the easiest.

Things have changed again, causing us to ask, "What is God's plan?" We have just found out that Mijo has tuberculosis and probably needs to stay in Port Moresby for several more months.

The doctor knew she had a spot on her lungs when she entered the hospital but couldn't treat it because her other health issues were more important. It has been difficult for her, and we have to cling to God's promises. We have to pray for a miracle and ask God what he has in mind for us."

Mijo was discharged in March 1967 and was back at work immediately. Adriaan relates that she was thrilled to be involved again after five months of absence. She soon was busy giving vaccinations as an epidemic of whooping cough was spreading across the region. While in the Mbuwa area, she took the time to write about the situation.

"This sickness is going from valley to valley. Women come in from far away valleys, up to two days walk, with children in their net bags along with their sweet potatoes."

All this tells us something of the mettle of the woman who had gone through so much herself yet could only think of helping others to bring glory to God.

The Ndugas Learn

During Mijo's setback, the only thing to do was to keep on working. The Bible Schools throughout the region need supervision. There was a Mapnduma Witness School to establish and staff to train evangelists to reach out into the villages with the gospel. The Ndugas were asked to choose couples with the potential to become future church leaders. The Witness School was modelled after the one in the Ilaga among the Damals where Mary Owen taught. Twenty-three couples entered the first Mapnduma Witness School. They were taught basic literacy and a Bible verse with a Bible story and a biblical lesson. In the evening the students spent hours at the missionaries' homes memorizing the Bible story word for word.

This method incorporated the natural talent for story-telling found in non-literate societies. On Fridays, right after school, the Witness Men would branch out to nearby villages and valleys to teach their people what they had learned. It was thrilling to hear the men leave on their evangelistic weekends singing their Nduga chants as they trekked over the mountains. Bible truths were set to Nduga tunes by the people themselves. They prayed powerful prayers which no doubt delighted the heart of God.

People in each village would gather to hear the Bible lesson several times during the weekend. They gathered early on Saturday morning before going to their gardens to dig sweet potatoes for Saturday and Sunday. The same story was taught in the men's houses on Saturday evening and in church services on Sunday. The Sunday offerings, consisting almost entirely of garden produce, were given to the men who delivered the gospel message. Many followed the Lord and truth was being received and making its impact. Those were exciting days in Ndugaland!

> "One of the Witness Men was Lomogolibaga. We called him L. He had a chief-like appearance and was a stately and respected leader. One night he dreamt that a man sat beside him and warned him not to take his bows and arrows. Then the man pointed his finger up toward the sky and said, "The talk that will be forever is up there." L realized that God was warning him not to take revenge in several ruthless circumstances."

When L heard that Wukun, his close friend, was near death, he hurried over the rough mountain trails to the sick man's village. Wukun's relatives speculated that the evil spirits were angry because they had turned Christian and so they were contemplating doing spirit worship. As the family pondered why Wukun was dying, L prayed:

> "O God, you only are great. You only are the Chief of our lives. You look right into our insides and know our thoughts. Heavenly Father, you know why my friend is so sick. O Father, please reach down and make him well so that he can work carefully in your garden. In Jesus' name, Amen."

Saturday evening his friend died. L's friends taunted him and began gathering firewood for the cremation. L continued to pray, "Lord, you made Lazarus come back to life. With your resurrection power, you can raise my friend."

> "It was Sunday evening. Darkness was beginning to fall at Mapnduma. From our upstairs window, we saw a noisy crowd gathering near our house. We hurried down to investigate. An overjoyed L was there with his now restored friend Wukun. They had come a day's walk over the mountains to show us that persistent prayer works. God heals. It is always too soon to quit."

While L was in the Mapnduma Witness School, he heard that a hostile group had killed his older sister. Filled with anger and resentment, and in a bewildered state of mind, he grabbed his bow and arrows and headed down the trail. Suddenly the picture of what the Lord Jesus had done for him on the cross flashed before him, and he remembered Jesus' words, "Vengeance is mine, I will repay." He stopped in his tracks and returned to Mapnduma. That evening he came to Adriaan's living room a humble man. He confessed his sin, repented, and left it all in God's hands.

During Witness School vacations, the Witness Men would travel to distant valleys to take the gospel message to Ndugas who had never heard it. While on one of these trips, L and a few other men sensed God leading them to take the gospel to the cannibals in the Wosak Valley. They arrived in Wandama and were warned not to go. L would not be dissuaded. He said, "I'm going. God wants us to go, and he is with us." With that, they were on their way. Suddenly a bright light shone from the mountain which confirmed to them that God was with them. L recounts the story:

"It took us two days hard trekking, and as we entered the area, we sang and saw people running for their bows and arrows and then coming toward us. When they saw that we were unarmed and wore clothes, they greeted us. One man in our group, Yaya, understood their dialect, so we spent two days there teaching them the gospel. On the third day, Yaya overheard them talking about getting cannibals from other villages and having a feast. We fled before they arrived. We travelled so fast over those mountain trails that it took us only one night to return when it had taken us two strenuous days to get there. We heard later that the cannibals were very angry that we had spoiled their feast."

Damage Control

The reality of sharing the transforming work of Christ in another culture is that counterfeit Christianity knows no boundaries. Adriaan discovered that some Ndugas had learned the proper answers to the questions when being examined for baptism but their lives revealed a lack of understanding.

"Deep in their heart, they believed that baptism would give them the right to go to heaven. They would never tell you this and probably can give the right answer if you ask the questions in the catechism booklet. However, if you ask questions not in the booklet, many times they do not know what to say. Everything is still so new for them."

Adriaan had to rely totally on God's guidance as he screened candidates for baptism. The cultural practices of the past when a man takes a second wife or a man beats his wife, needed to be put away. Much prayer and discipleship was needed.

The confrontation came to a head one Easter Sunday as they prepared for a baptismal service. As the team went through the names of candidates, they deleted several names for that reason. When one man found out that he could not be baptized, he was so infuriated that he went to the baptismal site at the river and destroyed it. With bow and arrows in hand, he shouted, "Me too, or nobody will be baptized."

> "I immediately went to control the damage and take him away. Only later did I realize that I could have been shot. We held the service at the river as planned. A big group of people with bows and arrows arrived, shouting and shooting arrows into the air. They frightened many, but we prayed, resisted the enemy, and continued with the baptism."

Responsibilities multiplied. Adriaan was coordinating five Bible Schools throughout Papua. Each Bible School had a different language and training needed to be done in the student's native language.

Trails and travel filled Adriaan's week. On his way through the Jigi Valley, Adriaan preached but also treated many yaws patients. Long-acting penicillin cleared up this tropical infection of the skin, bones and joints in seven to ten days and infected people migrated to Adriaan for help.

> "We recalled the time when several concerned Witness School students came to us. Nggweak, a young man from Jal, had come for medical help. Men from our Witness School came to inform us that Elfrieda was not to treat him for his yaws because his village had been involved in killing one of their relatives."

Nggweak had yaws with a foul-smelling ulcer on his leg. He was amazed when the ulcers on many of his friends cleared up after Adriaan treated them with just one injection. Nggweak's father, the Village Chief, was resistant to the gospel and cautioned his people not to accept the new talk. Nggweak, however, could not stand the stench and rejection of his disease any longer and made his way to Mapnduma for treatment.

The Witness School men confronted Nggweak about the murder of their relative, and after telling him about the Lord Jesus, they permitted Elfrieda to treat him. However, they added, "If you accept the Jesus talk, the ulcer will heal. If you don't, it won't." After treatment, they told him the story of Jairus' daughter who was healed. Then Nggweak left for his village.

> "Two weeks went by. There was a knock on our door. A large group of people from Nggweak's village had arrived asking for yaws treatment. They also asked if a pastor could come to their village to teach them the gospel. This amazing God-given medical tool had opened the hearts of the unbelievers in that village to accept the gospel. God works in marvellous ways, his wonders to perform.
>
> Next week it will be four years since we began our work here among the Ndugas. We have set an offensive against the forces of evil, seen sick healed, fetishes burned and miracles taking place. What a difference from before, when they had wars and murders, and contact with evil spirits, with some having the power to inflict damage or control over others. They talk about this when they get together to eat their sweet potato lunches."

A Moment's Reflection

On a somewhat quiet day, Adriaan had a few moments for contemplation. He sat in his office, looking out his window. They had come a long way.

> "I see the airstrip with the deep ravines and thick rain clouds overhead. I hear thunder—more rain is coming. I also hear the noise of the wild river. The garden looks nice with roses and other tropical flowers. We are so thankful for what the Lord has given us and for the joy we have as we serve these people."

There was a yearning voice inside him that seemed to say, "Maybe life can be normal for a while." But the thought is not even voiced. He looks around him again.

> "There is such a contrast between rich and poor. Here we live in a castle, figuratively speaking, and a few hundred yards away, the people live in their huts. Will there ever be a time that they might build a house like ours, or eat the same food as we do? But then, there is the promise of John 14:2, 3, with Jesus saying: My Father's house has many rooms; if that were not so, would I have told you that I am going there to prepare a place for you? And if I go and prepare a place for you, I will come back and take you to be with me that you also may be where I am. It must be wonderful for them to believe that day will come for those who have trusted in him."

Adriaan was conscious of how accustomed he had become to living close to the lip of disaster when, while coming home from a conference in Ilaga Valley, the front wheel of the plane broke as they landed in Mapnduma. The plane sat on the runway for a month until the parts could be flown in from the United States.

They were often at the mercy of the elements and mechanical failure. Rainy season comes to Ndugaland during May through August. It is a cloudy time with much rainfall, which often prevents planes from landing in Mapnduma. They learned to take the weather and its limitations in stride.

But there were times when good weather, and skillful pilots, and planes in good repair combined to pull off the spectacular. They were at the Field

Conference in Pyramid. Mijo was about to give birth to their youngest son, Paul. They could not get medical help in Pyramid and decided to fly to the hospital at Pit River. She had been having contractions for twenty-four hours before they were able to get a flight.

> "Although it was getting dark, we flew on to Pit River. As we were landing, we could see the fires outlining the end of the strip so the pilot could see where to land."

God held them safe in his hands and his perfect timing. The plane landed on the airstrip in time for Paul to be born under the guidance of a capable doctor.

It was another just-in-time confluence of divine orchestration. Once again what seems like high drama to most was recalled matter-of-factly. In Ndugland, this was everyday fare.

The Compass Deflects

A squall that threatened to blow them off course was soon to come. Mijo was tired from the flights and the constant pressure of her role in attending to the health needs of the Ndugas day and night. It was not a good time to throw a curve into her world.

But it came through the voice of constituted authority: We would like you to consider leaving Mapnduma to serve as house parents at the mission boarding school for children. Mission leaders at the annual Field Conference believed that Adriaan and Mijo would be the best choice for manning the school in Sentani.

"We've just gotten a toehold in the door to the Ndugas," they argued.

"You have three school-age children," they countered, assuming that playing the motherhood card might sway them.

Mijo realized they were desperate, but she also knew what it had cost her to get to where she now was. The thought of babysitting a dorm of children did not appeal to her.

"We have no one else," the voice of the assembled conference explained. "Would you consider doing it for one year?"

After prayer, Adriaan and Mijo made their decision: We'll do it. We have to get used to this kind of life.

Daniel, Adriaan, Paul, Heidi, Mijo, David

When people come to the mission field, their compass is so fixed on their calling that the occasional detours are only temporary inconveniences. It can take you a more circuitous route to get to the destination, but it does not alter the end goal. Their focus was fixed like a north star that would not be deterred by these minor disruptions.

Running a boarding school for missionary children was no picnic, but they did it without complaint.

Another Detour

During the time Adriaan and Mijo were at the MK school, more than 300 Ndugas had been baptized by an ordained national. Adriaan observed that the Ndugas showed more discernment than ever before about the significance of baptism and the requirements for baptism. In their absence, Mary and Elfrieda had continued the teaching load in the Mapnduma Witness School. There was no time to waste. They had been away from Mapnduma for the school year, but they were still a year away from their international leave. They couldn't wait to join the action.

> "Our goal was to start a Bible School for the Ndugas to replace the Witness School. Mary Owen focused on completing the translation of the Gospel of Luke in mimeographed form. I would be doing a good share of the teaching. We were delighted when Sion Bible School opened with twenty couples in the fall of 1969. Students in each Bible School class studied for three years and were much better prepared to disciple the people in the village churches than they were in the Witness School. Graduations were joyful occasions."

Mijo was to be tested again. During her annual physical examination, Mijo's doctor discovered a breast lump. The biopsy tissue was sent to Australia for analysis. It took three long months of waiting before the biopsy report arrived. It was positive. A quick decision was made to return to Holland. Instead of joining in the new venture, they were once again on the sidelines.

> "For our family, it was a time of stress and uncertainty. Mary came to sit with Mijo. As they talked about the diagnosis of cancer, Mijo began to sing, It Is Well with My Soul. Singing her life song at a time like this affirmed her deep, enduring faith in God."

They had one day to hand over their responsibilities, pack their suitcases, fly to Sentani to pick up their children from MK School, and leave for Holland.

Elfrieda wore sunglasses as she waved goodbye when the plane took off. The dark glasses hid her tears as she empathized with Mijo, only thirty-four years-old, coping with yet another health crisis. For someone so committed to Ndugaland, she was having a hard time staying.

6

HOME AGAIN

Mijo was admitted to the hospital in October 1969 wondering what purpose God had to take her so far away from her beloved Ndugas. While there, she got acquainted with the woman in the next bed and was able to tell her about God's love. The woman accepted Christ as her Saviour. A few days later, she died. Mijo realized that leading this woman to Jesus was one reason why she had to undergo this ordeal.

During surgery, the doctor removed her right breast as well as the cancerous tumour. When the adjacent lymph nodes were removed, the surrounding area on her left arm was compromised. It remained swollen and red and for the rest of her life she wore long-sleeved outfits to keep her arms covered.

To their delight, in June 1971 during Mijo's follow-up medical evaluation, she received clearance to return to ministry in Ndugaland. On June 22, 1971, they were in the air flying toward Papua.

When Adriaan and Mijo arrived home in Mapnduma, they were thrilled to find many new churches established. In distant valleys, ten churches were opened and five preaching centers established. They had reached the outer limits of the Nduga tribal boundaries. Still, many valleys were difficult to reach, which meant that some villages had never been visited.

Martyrs for Christ

The distant Wosak Valley with its many unreached villages was a concern. Back in the Mapnduma Witness School days, an evangelistic team of ten men from the Witness School, Jigi Valley, and the Iniye Valley volunteered to go into the treacherous Kora and Wosak Valleys. They knew the trails would be difficult especially when the rains came. They also knew they might be hungry because they would be trekking through uninhabited areas. Before they left, they repeated the vow of devotion to Christ common to evangelists in Papua.

> "We are ready to be killed for you,
>   to drown or be crushed in a landslide in your service.
>   You died for us.
>   Your servant Paul went through great tribulations for you.
>   We are ready to suffer for you, too."

The ten evangelists travelled through the Jigi Valley, where a large group, including several chiefs, joined them. They moved through the Mbuwa Valley and on to the Iniye. Beyond the Iniye was no-man's-land and valleys to be claimed for the Lord—the Kora and the Wosak.

Entering the valleys close by the Kora, the party met local men from the area who gave them little encouragement. Every day they asked God to shield them from danger and thanked him for his protection over them. In need of food, they worked in the gardens of the Kora people to pay for sweet potatoes. Announcing their intention to penetrate deeper into the valley, they were advised not to go. Later they learned that a large group of warriors had laid an ambush to kill them.

Hungry, and discouraged by continuous rains, they pushed on toward the Wosak. There was very little traffic between those valleys, and the trails, as steep as the walls of their houses, hardly deserved the name. They had to use both hands and feet to make progress.

They came to the top of a mountain where the only possible descent was down a steep and narrow riverbed made more difficult by a recent landslide. The men divided into smaller groups, each group picking its way down the precipitous slope slowly.

As the final group began their descent, they saw a landslide in the making, and hastily retreated. The groups farther down the gorge had no refuge.

Boulders started to roll. Mud loosened by the continuous rain began to shift. As the slide gained momentum, trees were uprooted, and an enormous wall of debris plummeted down the gorge.

The men below, partially deafened by the rain on the rain mats they were wearing, heard the piercing cries of their companions. They scrambled up the steep walls, grasping grass, roots, and rock—anything that would protect them from the wild fury of mud, water, rocks, and trees sweeping by beneath their feet. Some were struck by hurling stones and whipping branches.

Obadja, a Witness Man, was carrying a metal phonograph in his net bag. His companions, startled when a log struck the box with a thud, turned to see a tree lift Obadja into the air and sweep him away. Those lower in the valley saw body parts come by and feared the worst.

When the noise subsided, and the men could gather, eight were missing. Another was seriously injured. Part of his foot was severed and his shoulder dislocated.

Those who survived had escaped only with their lives. Their possessions carried in the net bags on their backs had been swept away. All were barely recognizable because of the mud which had splashed over them. It was a miracle anyone was still alive. They took shelter in a deserted Wosak house near a village, huddling together in speechless fear and awe.

Villagers found them and showed friendly sympathy, commiserating with them on the loss of their friends and bringing them food. The next day the villagers killed pigs and prepared a feast as a token of acceptance. Their friendliness was a great comfort.

Word of the tragedy spread fast through the valleys. Early reports reaching Adriaan and the Mapnduma team were conflicting. Had it been a landslide or were the men murdered by hostile tribesmen? Later details in all their chilling horror confirmed the truth of the landslide.

> "With what sorrow we mingled our tears with the family and friends of Obadja's young widow. We grieved with the loved ones of the other seven who lost their lives. In the midst of all our sorrow comes the glorious vision of those eight messengers of the cross, dressed in white robes as they surround the throne praising the Lamb who was slain for them.
>
> Eight new Papuan martyrs join others who have given their lives for the spread of the gospel in these dark, unreached valleys. May grace be given us to follow in their train."

The reaction of the loved ones varied, but the response of the Jigi people was most encouraging:

> "We have committed our loss to God. Because our blood has been shed in the Wosak it has become our land, and we will continue to take the gospel there."

We Want to be Friends!

In January 1972, Adriaan went into the same area with a Nduga group and was blessed to see how God had prepared the people.

> "When I got to one of the villages in the Wosak Valley, two large

groups had gathered. One group shouted: We used to kill you and drink from your skulls. The other group responded: We stole your women and pigs and left your villages in flames! But now we want to be friends!

With a shout of joy, the opposing groups ran together. They merged into one huge group, dancing and singing praises to God that he had made them one in Christ. It was a living demonstration of what the love of God can and will do when even cannibals put away their vile ways. Witnessing that moment was worth every step of the treacherous trip."

Throughout the year, the Mapnduma team saw God moving among the tribes. About 500 people were baptized that year.

Growing Pains

The people in Mapnduma had learned to read, creating a demand for devotionals, Bible study helps, Sunday School lessons, and the Scriptures in their language. This placed new demands on the team.

The Sion Bible School, with fifty couples enrolled in two classes, was stretched to capacity. There was not enough space to accommodate them, as well as a lack of space to grow sweet potatoes, and therefore, a lack of available food. Many students and their families went hungry for days.

"I began to wonder how wise it was to conduct two classes at a time. The national teachers were doing a good job despite the very minimal salary of four dollars a month.

For some time, the Nduga tribe had struggled with poor crops. By 1972, about 800 people had moved down south to Keneyam, an area where they anticipated they would be able to survive better. We knew that they would encounter other difficult problems in the warmer climate, and that we would have to help them.

The people would need directions on how to plant different varieties of plants. Could the malaria problem be solved? With all these challenges I knew I would be called on for advice and practical help."

The Church Celebrates

Preparations had been made for months for the 1972 Puncak Conference. This was a highlight for the Nduga church, which encompassed the central part of the Papua field. It would be held in Mapnduma for the first time.

> "People had planted more potatoes than usual, cleaned up the station, enlarged and painted the church and worked to earn money to purchase rice. Then, because of a severe drought, the gardens did not produce as expected. As a result, many people sacrificed for the conference, going hungry for many days, so they could save their produce to feed the delegates."

The big day arrived, and the delegates began to pour in. Many walked the trails while others flew in. More than 2,000 Ndugas gathered, the largest gathering ever of people from this tribe in Mapnduma.

> "We saw a demonstration of oneness during the conference. People from the Wosak Valley in the east to the Pulpa Valley in the west stood together. With great shouts, they stood firm in their decision to do away with the old life and live together in the new life, including doing away with the bride price. On the last day, they roasted 300 pigs for the feast."

After the feast, everyone left as soon as possible so that the hosts would not have so many to feed. The airstrip was very busy with nearly forty landings.

Help Needed!

The pressures mounted. The aftermath of the opening of the Freeport Mining Company far to the west had Ndugas talking about getting hired, enticed by all the benefits they could expect. Because of the enormous distances in the Nduga area, Adriaan could not visit enough to satisfy the people. His involvement in Sion Bible School made additional trekking unrealistic.

> "We need another missionary couple to join us. Area wise our region is bigger than the entire Baliem Valley. It covers seventy by thirty-five miles over very rough terrain. While we plan to develop

more airstrips, much trekking is still required. People need to be discipled and there is just too much ministry for us to do adequately with the limited staff we have."

Looking back over the work with the Nduga tribe, the church now numbered about 7,000 people after ten years. About fifty churches had been established. The Nduga tribe had aggressively reached out to others. Among their own people they had evangelized from the Alama Valley in the west to the Wosak Valley in the east. The dream was that once these fifty churches had trained pastors, they could send out evangelists to other tribes.

"Although these years had been years of fast expansion, I was concerned that the depth of their spiritual experience had not kept pace.

The crowning event of 1972 was the graduation of the first class of the Sion Bible School. Begun in 1969, twenty-one of the original twenty-eight couples had graduated. Both Elfrieda and Mary taught in the Bible School. Still, despite the high returns on our efforts only eighteen churches had Bible School graduates as pastors."

Nduga teachers were to do some of the teaching, yet because of tight family ties it is sometimes difficult for a national teacher to discipline or train students. The students were not willing to accept the national teacher as an authority figure. For that reason, Adriaan anticipated that a missionary would very likely always have to be on the faculty.

Highs and Lows

The watershed of Nduga growth had been reached by 1973. On the positive side of the ledger, the Keneyam area was developing. The Prep School, which prepared Nduga leaders to learn Indonesian so they could attend an Indonesian Bible School, was relocated from Mapnduma to the Keneyam area. The airstrip opened on November 20 and roads were being built. A village public hall was constructed. Around 600-800 people had moved into the area and still more people were moving from the upper valleys. Adriaan expressed his concern that government involvement might not be in the best interest of the Ndugas.

> "Although the government was interested in opening a post there, I had mixed feelings about this move, aware of the dangers of malaria and other challenges that the Ndugas would face."

The only solution was for evangelism to outstrip the intrusion from outside. To reach the whole tribe there was need for more airstrips. The Keneyam airstrips in the low lands, at 400 feet elevation, and the Jigi strip at 5700 feet were opened. Work was underway in the rugged Wosak Valley. Because of the lack of airstrips, Adriaan could do nothing else but resort to hiking the trails.

"I did extensive trekking this year and ministered throughout the Nduga area, walking into the Wosak twice, several times to the Keneyam area, as well as treks into the Iniye, Mbuwa and Jigi Valleys."

The results of that sacrifice and dedication were noticeable.

"By the end of 1973, 965 people were baptized. In Mapnduma, people burned their fetishes demonstrating a fresh dedication to God."

Yet, the challenges never stopped. When the first graduates from the Indonesian Prep school learned that the flight prices were too high to fly out to attend the Kebo Bible School, they decided not to attend.

Health issues had been precipitated when people moved from a cool climate to Keneyam's warmer temperatures. People were developing enlarged spleens and coping with malaria. Although there was an abundance of food and other things, which had motivated the move, a shortage of medication was now a critical factor.

"A shipment of 60,000 malaria pills lost from the Schultzs' outfit was a real blow as they are not easily replaced. I began to question the wisdom of the move. Now what should be done?"

The medical work led by Elfrieda continued to expand, but she was not receiving the additional medicines to help the people as new clinics were built in the Keneyam and in the Jigi. Construction supervision continued to fall on Adriaan's plate. Without a carpenter who knew how to handle the square and level well, church construction remained one of his jobs. Many churches had started to gather money for aluminum roofs, which meant that the roofs would need to be rebuilt. The aluminum nails and other supplies to rebuild a roof would have to be flown in.

"To earn money to pay for the roofing materials, people have to trek four to five days to Wamena to sell their pigs. As nice as aluminum roofs and improved buildings are, I had hoped that there would be a desire to be revived as living stones, built into a spiritual house with Christ as the Builder."

Another concern was the lack of biblical knowledge among the youth. Some of the young men were learning about the traditions from their past and going back to the customs of their forefathers, letting their hair grow again and greasing themselves up to reveal externally the signs of their inner conflict.

When Adriaan made the trek to the Wosak to open the airstrip, he was disappointed to report that it was not up to standard.

> "Because it is located in such an awkward spot, I wondered if it would ever meet the standard. We hope with some more work that MAF will consent to land on it, so it might be used a few times in the coming years."

In the end it became MAF's largest and most expensive helicopter pad in Papua!

The Bottom Line

The spiritual situation of these valleys remained the greatest concern. Catholics working in the area did not say anything against having two wives and eating pigs for the dead. The people liked the gospel and the presence of preachers in their villages, but still persisted in traditions of the old life.

> "We needed to see depth in the spiritual life before we could conduct more baptisms. As a result, only a few people were baptized in the Akimuga area.
>
> I prayed that the Lord would work among the leaders in the Nduga church so that we again would see the miracle-working power we saw when we started the work ten years earlier. My deep desire continued to be that his name would again be glorified in the hearts and lives of these men and women to be tools in the building up of his church in this area.
>
> There are still areas, such as the Kora area, that need a visit and the dialect is very different. The terrain in that area is difficult,

making trekking into it challenging, but they also need to know the freedom that can only be found in Christ."

The months ahead were laden with conferences and meetings. Mel Tari and Frans Selan who had come out of the revival from the Indonesian island of Timor were the speakers. God moved mightily in many hearts. A crowning event was the pig feast where around 350 pigs were killed—a very large feast for the valleys south of the ranges.

Several of the unresponsive chiefs from the Inije and Mbuwa Valleys attended the feast, and the church leaders took full advantage of the occasion to present the claims of Christ to those recalcitrant leaders of Nduga society. The believers faithfully prayed for these chiefs both in their monthly day of prayer and fasting and in their private prayer times.

Decision Time

By 1975, despite the good growth, Mijo and Adriaan had made a major decision. The needs around them were everywhere, yet they left for a scheduled furlough in Holland with mixed feelings. Their hearts were torn between their love of family and concern for the welfare of the Ndugas. They were not sure when they would be back.

It would be seven years before they returned. Their ultimate destiny had not wavered and their compass was still set on the nations. They were responsible for Mijo's mother and they needed extended time to attend to the needs of their four children.

> "We have the desire to return to the mission field, but it seems impossible, due to visa issues with Indonesia. We need to know the Lord's will."

The van der Bijls had their answer when on August 14, 1982 their permanent visas were granted. Their departure flights were scheduled for the morning of August 19.

7

MILESTONES

WHEN THE VAN DER BIJLS LANDED at the Sentani Airport on August 26, 1982, they were welcomed with great joy by the Sentani family. Then it was on to Mapnduma. Mary and Elfrieda were on home assignment but had left behind some basic provisions for guests who might arrive. Perhaps they had thought that the next to arrive might be Adriaan, Mijo and family.

Loose ends clamoured for immediate attention. It didn't take long for the Ndugas to begin asking for financial help. The first request was for money to purchase new uniforms for the high school and university students at the coast. It would soon escalate to epidemic proportions.

"I do not think we are wise to give the students all that money. They should be taught to earn it for themselves. The people in Mapnduma should take some responsibility.

I will be able to get the students sponsored by a Christian businessman in Germany at the beginning of the year to the tune of twenty dollars a month. However, they should find jobs to get at least some pocket money.

Of course, I know that you will never get 100% results, and I am happy with the teachers that we have now but let us be careful not to make them into educated beggars. I also feel now that, in the future, we should be selective in what students we pick to go on to higher education at Abepura University at the coast. Only the ones who have proven themselves should go.

Linus was one of those. He excelled in his studies and lived out his faith at school. After graduation, he went back to his home in Ndugaland to teach more than one hundred children in grades one through six from the surrounding villages in the Jigi Valley."

Adriaan did an additional assessment of the state of the school program. He believed it would not be wise to make future student residences exclusively Nduga. Other areas like the Puncak District were asking for schools. In the future, districts would have to help in building their dorms. This was his reasoning.

"I raised interest again with two Dutch radio stations for this project. They would be far more open to contributing if we do not make it that exclusive."

Adriaan drew up a dorm plan to house thirty to sixty boys. He recognized the need for education. He was not quite sure how to get there.

There was another anomaly. No rain. Planes could not fly because of the smog from thousands of fires everywhere.

"It seems like a disaster. We have almost used all the rainwater in our drums and will have to go back to water from the stream which we hooked up and piped into the bathroom. Very strange weather, which is frightening."

Reality had set in. They were getting into the swing again with all the blessings and woes that came with it.

A Letter from Mijo

In February, Mijo penned a letter to Elfrieda who was still home on furlough that expressed her feelings for what it meant to be home in Mapnduma finally. It is a heartfelt, honest evaluation of what they had done among the Ndugas and what was yet to be done.

"I still feel like in a dream when I look down from our house and see the whole valley! The Lord has done great things to bring us back among the Ndugas. I feel so unworthy that my Lord should do so much for us. In many ways, it is like we never went away. So many things are the same, while others have not much changed.

We believe that our coming back to the field has more to do with the Ndugas themselves than with ourselves. For some reason, the Lord ordained it. We will know someday. My heart was always here, yet, I didn't think that we were of much help to the people, except maybe some kind of an emotional figure that gave them some status with the other tribes since they are no longer the last cucumber on the vine. But maybe there is more to it.

The way they welcomed us, in tears, moved us deeply. We know that we belong here even if we are not as efficient and talented as many missionaries here. Daily, we are experiencing what Paul says: When I am weak, I am strong! What the Lord does through our little us, is great and mighty, just because it is him and not us. It is much better that way. And because of that, we have a great assurance in our hearts, that it is the place that the Lord has prepared even before we were born that we should walk in it! We believe that the Lord has a special goal for us, to have brought us back, and we want to know what it is. It is not to build the church. Jesus is the builder. We just pray that the Lord will give us a free spirit to face whatever it is he has ordained."

Mijo then went on to assess the medical needs and challenges as she observed them after seven years away from Mapnduma. There were the normal frustrations of bad weather (too dry or cloudy), cancelled flights, hunger, and then sickness!

"The last two weeks we had nine deaths at Mapnduma. Before this epidemic, we had the measles going around. Now it is an amoebic dysentery outbreak.

The upper valleys, Jigi and Mbuwa, counted forty deaths. Adriaan came back from a trip there and said they are hungry people, too weak to fight the sickness. The government has been helpful and has already provided rice a few times!

Elf, may the Lord be very close to you, We love you. Shalom! Mijo"

A Few Observations

Annual conferences in Irian Jaya provided the necessary format for evaluation and recommendations to the larger body including colleagues and field leaders. Adriaan's thoughtful analysis became the significant fodder for what he was thinking, and how he had evaluated the work in his area of responsibility.

It was a forthright observation of how Adriaan saw the church with the perspective of a seven-year absence.

> "We praise the Lord for bringing us back to Irian Jaya to serve again among the Ndugas, and for miraculously granting us a visa to come back into this country."

There were some foundational premises that Adriaan worked out in his own mind.

> "First, this work is God's work and however we feel about it is of little importance. He has built his church among these people and is continuing to add to those who want to follow him."

The church existed. There was no way to minimize its existence in this isolated place.

> "When we see things that seem so different from what we think a church should be, we need to remind ourselves that it might be immaterial to how God sees them through Jesus Christ. We believe that the timing and even the necessity of our return fits into the picture of how God already views his church among them.
>
> We believe that our return has sparked a new hope and we want to be aware of the needs, especially the spiritual ones."

There were encouraging signs that their presence had brought new optimism to the region.

> "Recently, we had the dedication of a new church building in Mapnduma when possibly 2,000 Ndugas from many valleys converged for the big event."

Adriaan and Mijo observed the enthusiasm demonstrated by the Ndugas dancing in full native array of feather headdress and body paint. Following the dancing, the dedication service took place ending the day with the customary service and pig feast. What a royal welcome back!

Further cultural issues that distracted from full surrender to God surfaced the day after the dedication when the subject of the bride price came up, and a fight broke out between the two factions about this issue.

> "No one was hurt, but it showed us that there are many deep-rooted feelings still lingering from long, long ago.
>
> Although the gospel has brought a general peace and stability, the slightest spark of discontentment rebuilds the old barriers which existed before the gospel arrived. Much prayer and Holy Spirit directed guidance are needed to teach them to live in unity."

The presence of dissidents moving more freely through the highlands was also a widening concern. They were advocates of local independence and instigators of unrest. Adriaan admired and recognized the ministry of Mary Owen and Elfrieda Toews who were here alone for so long. He felt responsible for some of the difficult situations the women had faced. In the Nduga culture male leadership is essential. He summarized his report by adding that many misunderstandings and hard feelings could have been avoided if a man had given leadership.

Looking Back

As he prepared to write his 1983 Annual Field Conference Report, Adriaan reviewed the past twenty years of Nduga ministry.

> "The airstrip at Mapnduma was ready for use within five weeks. In all these years, we have had no accidents, even with Mapnduma's bad weather reputation. The Mbuwa, Wandama, Keneyam and Jigi also have airstrips, a tremendous help in moving around this vast area.
>
> From a few small churches when we first came to Mapnduma, to almost fifty now, the Nduga church has been established in many valleys. The workers are now trained in the Sion Bible

School, started as a Witness School in 1965. So much has been accomplished through God's faithful guidance."

The helicopter was a wonderful, but expensive, answer to the difficult trail problem, but the Nduga people highly valued Adriaan's hours of trekking with them back and forth to the villages.

Adriaan also noted the strong medical work among the Ndugas.

"It is one of the best organized on the field due to the tremendous abilities of Elfrieda Toews. Beginning with two young Nduga men in 1964, it has grown to eighty medical workers. The women are now well trained in midwifery, women and children's health. Our medical workers have been assigned to thirty-five clinics throughout the twelve Nduga Valleys. Several medical workers have medical status with the Indonesian government and are receiving salaries. Despite many difficulties—the lack of medicines, epidemics, and large areas to be covered—we have seen a marked improvement in the general health of the people. Malaria will always be the main cause of death among the Nduga tribe, especially in the lower valleys."

Because Adriaan was responsible for food distribution, he saw something that pained him.

"When drought and famine hit the area, pots, cooking oil, and more than fifty sacks of rice were flown in. The selfishness of our starving people caused me a lot of problems and headaches as I tried to distribute the rice fairly. After that, a flu epidemic swept through our valleys and caused more than 200 deaths, mostly among children."

Ten years earlier, he had written in a report:

"These coming years should see less involvement of the white missionary, working towards a strong, independent, self-supporting, self-governing and self-propagating church. Healthy and happy will be the day that we can pull up stakes, leaving behind a church ready for the coming of the Lord. We are well aware that much teaching and concentrated discipleship are still needed in a culture so fresh out of the Stone Age."

How I See It

More time in Mapnduma gave Adriaan a clearer picture of the challenge before them. In another Conference Report, he had a full year of ministry to report, as well as a look back at the twenty years since the work began in

Mapnduma. The two reports together give a succinct picture of their happy return to Mapnduma, the present reality of the church, and the spiralling down of spiritual fervour.

"This year is the twentieth anniversary year of the Nduga church. It was Reformation Day, October 31, 1963, that the first Nduga missionary set foot in Mapnduma, the center of activity in the coming years. We praise the Lord for the marvellous growth and strength the church among the Ndugas has shown throughout these twenty years. Anniversary celebrations, planned for the end of October, were rescheduled to the end of January 1984. The crowning event of these celebrations will be the presentation of the Nduga New Testament, the result of Mary Owen's twenty years of diligent and unswerving work. It is now on press at the Indonesian Bible Society in Bogor, Indonesia. The Ndugas will so welcome this book, and it will be an especially satisfying moment for Mary Owen, who has so faithfully worked all these years toward this moment."

Adriaan summarized the activities in 1983 to give his mission team an understanding of the ministry year. This report gives a snapshot of their year. It also gives a blow-by-blow look at the complexity of the world they had rejoined.

"Too much time was used to discuss church problems while spiritual fellowship was sadly neglected.

We visited several areas this year, including the Wosak, which is the farthest from Mapnduma, difficult to reach and the dialect hard to understand. The helicopter is a solution to this problem. A real necessity is to have another missionary couple there to disciple these people whose culture is so different from other Nduga valleys.

The Keneyam was visited after many years of neglect. It is in deplorable state with the church building fallen down and the people disheartened. The airstrip, which had been washed away, was lengthened again and hopefully, will be operational again for the Cessna airplane shortly.

There is a push from the government to settle people in the lowlands. It is doubtful if this area can ever be liveable for the mountain people. Experience has taught us that no one should be forced or enticed to move there. It should be voluntary.

People of the Wosak have started to make a clearing in the jungle lowlands by the name of Geyarik. It will take work and patience to hack out an airstrip, but the site seems well located and suitable.

This year we have seen little activity by the dissidents. It seems that many have grown weary of the hardships of living in the jungle. There is still a core of several hundred who are holding out.

There were very few baptisms this year. The church is at low ebb with the area so widespread it is hard to oversee, disciple and encourage them. Many are returning to their old habits again—witchcraft, taking second wives, reviving old problems of many years ago, wars and rumours of wars.

A long war raged in the Jigi resulting in two deaths and many wounded. It has now settled into an uneasy peace, but the heart of the problem is unwillingness to recognize selfishness as sin. They have settled into a mediocre and uncommitted way of life."

The never-ending myriad responsibilities continued. Adriaan resumed his teaching load at the Sion Bible School. He needed to expedite a community development program which World Vision was funding in the Nduga area. Animals, seeds and medicines were purchased. A bridge-building program was underway. A sewing course produced some well-trained tailors. This involved trips to the coast at Sentani to purchase bolts of material, thread, needles and scissors to supply the ladies with the essential items necessary for the course. Elfrieda always enjoyed going with her sister Elsie to the early morning market in Sentani to get in on the good deals for the sewing ladies at Mapnduma.

Ngget Tul Pidnak Wene—The New Promise Talk

The dedication of the Nduga New Testament in January 1984 was beyond question the highlight of Mapnduma's twentieth-anniversary events. The long-awaited Nduga Bible was a reality. Ngget Tul Pidnak Wene—The New Promise Talk—so enthusiastically embraced by the Ndugas, was especially meaningful to Mary Owen who invested so much prayer, energy and time to make it happen. The happy day made the past twenty years all worthwhile as she celebrated the arrival of Ngget Tul Pidnak Wene with the Ndugas.

> "It is gratifying to see pastors reading their New Testaments by the hour as they prepare their sermons. The Holy Spirit who inspired the Scriptures now inspires the pastors as they preach the Word with power."

Mary Owen was already an accomplished linguist when she began to study the Nduga language, putting it down on paper and teaching the people to read. Born in Toledo, Ohio she sailed to Netherlands New Guinea in 1957. She spent five years working with the Damal tribe before moving to Mapnduma.

The people were thrilled to have someone who cared about them enough to want to learn their language and teach them how to read and write it. Mary's first informants were young men from Hitadipa where years ago Adriaan received the little bundle of sticks with a request to become their missionary. The two informants, who had Damal mothers and Nduga fathers, became Mary's bridge to the Nduga language.

"Mary has already done quite a bit of translation work. We can now study the Nduga language better. It is rather difficult to make ourselves understood."

The Ndugas did not understand the word "God." So the name Mbal Pem Nagawan—The Chief of the Sky—was chosen. They had no exposure to bread, so it was natural to translate bread as sweet potato, their bread of life. Here is the translation of John 3:16 and how it reads in English:

English	*Nduga*	*Translation*
God so loved the world that he gave his one and only Son, that whoever believes in him shall not perish but have eternal life *John 3:16/NIV*	Mbal Pem Nagawan-nen ki nap pidsa nen-abuwa nggulok karuk, at Ambara misiget nderak wok nenda-mu-o. Ta-nen nde at ebem inndi angin tubu yuwa nab-e lak yigit lag-et, are, pem-et unlug-et woralik nalik momtak elem irit wanuwa-o.	The Chief of the Sky loved us real people so very much that he gave us his only Son. Whoever believes in him will not die but will receive life that will last forever.

Translating Scripture is a high calling. First on the list was the Book of Mark, translating, typing, and mimeographing each page. Then it was revised, again and again. This procedure was followed with each of the twenty-seven New Testament books. The Sion Bible School was an invaluable testing ground. Mimeographed copies of the Scriptures were used to teach the Bible courses and to determine if the translations were clear and understandable.

Painstakingly typing several error-free copies of the New Testament manuscript as required by the Indonesian Bible Society (IBS) on an old-style typewriter was a challenge. It was a joy-filled day when Mary delivered the manuscripts to the IBS office. Translations were checked for accuracy by IBS and then sent to the printer.

It was twenty-four months later that printed copies arrived in Mapnduma from the printer in Bogor, Indonesia. For years the Nudgas read God's Word on mimeographed sheets of paper. Then it became available as a series of books. Now it was all in one book. They were ecstatic! It was their very own Bible. Dedication day was a celebration like no other. The words of eternal life, a treasure of great worth, was theirs at last.

"The Ndugas made it clear that they also wanted the Old Testament in their language. They did not think the little Old Testament storybook we had translated years before was sufficient. So began the work on the Nanduk Tul Pidnak Wene—The Previous Promise Talk. We referred to it as the Shorter Old Testament. In Ndugaland, shorter means here and there."

Mary and Elias, her trusted co-translator, began to work on the Old Testament using the guidelines suggested by the American Bible Society, which leaves out repetitious parts of the Old Testament. Occasionally Elias would object to leaving out stories omitted by the American Bible Society. "We had that story in our little Old Testament storybooks. It has to be in the translation we are doing, or they will think we made those stories up."

The Shorter Old Testament was translated and printed much quicker, thanks to the addition of another team member. In 1987, Mary married Richard Byrne while on furlough in Ohio. The newlyweds arrived in Papua the following year. The marriage brought an important partner into the translation process. Dick's computer expertise enabled him to format the manuscript reducing the turnaround time significantly. Dick also prepared and published a Nduga concordance, another important contribution to the Nduga church.

The dedication of The Shorter Old Testament was at Hitadipa in 1992 where many Ndugas live. Later there was a dedication service at Mapnduma with the accompanying traditional pig feast, common to all celebrations.

The hard work, at times tedious, with the literacy program was evident. More than 400 Ndugas were learning to read. The excitement was high on the literacy front as pastors and their wives taught literacy classes. Ngge Yimin and Gideon, faithful helpers, travelled from village to village testing aspiring readers and, if they were ready, giving them the next primer in a series of six.

The effect of a single piece of literature has multiplied a hundredfold as the pastors span out over their valleys. It was never just a booklet on a shelf. It was a ministry in action. So important was the literature program to the

Ndugas that when they realized their missionaries would eventually retire to a life in North America, they wanted assurance that Nduga Bibles, manuals and booklets would remain with them in Ndugaland.

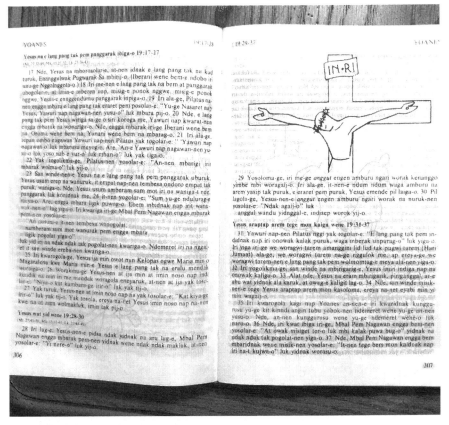

A Visitor from Brooklyn

It was an unanticipated event when Samuel, a Jewish anthropologist from Brooklyn, New York walked over the high ranges into Aser's village. His objective was to prove that missionaries were disrupting the culture of the Nduga people.

The Mbuwa people were thrilled to welcome Samuel to their village. He slept in the men's hut, ate their sweet potatoes and communicated with his English-Indonesian dictionary. He was intrigued with their interest in Ngget Tul Pidnak Wene as the people spent evening after evening reading their precious little book with the red cover.

While there, Samuel became ill. He was so sick he thought he was going to die. Medical worker Aser treated him at the clinic. He killed several of his chickens for Samuel to eat to help him regain his strength. When Samuel needed to leave to return to the United States, the Ndugas loaded him down with food for the trek. He had come to expose missionaries disrupting the culture. He left in awe. They were enhancing it.

On his way to the coastal city of Jayapura, he met Mary Owen. He told her about Aser and asked if he could buy a New Testament to see what made the Nduga people tick. He wanted one to remind him of how well they had treated him. This little book had bridged the gap between cultural barriers and touched the heart of a young Jewish anthropologist.

Looking Ahead

Bad weather had forced Adriaan to stay in the Wosak at their trailhouse for three days. There was nothing to do but wait it out. He used the time to write his 1984 Mapnduma report. The weather did little to lift his spirits as he penned the narrative. Perhaps it was the dismal climate that added to the gloom of the report, but this was not the typical Adriaan speaking. It was the least optimistic and most transparent expression of what Adriaan was feeling inside.

> "As I look out the window of our trailhouse, it looks dismal. Solid walls of fog make me wonder if I will ever get out of here. This kind of day is good for reflection and meditation, asking oneself how effective one's ministry is. I see people living in the same situation as they did twenty years ago. Several church buildings were constructed, which are used once a week. Some are rotting away because of leaky roofs due to the daily afternoon rains."

Like the leaking roofs, the spirituality of the church needed repair as well.

> "With the war dragging on for three years in the Wosak, the gospel does not seem to have made a lot of difference. If only more missionaries were available to give on-the-spot leadership and discipleship training in this spread-out tribe, there would be more evident fruit."

Another war sprang up in the Jigi with the same results—people putting their faith aside and returning to their old ways, saving family members rather than saving God's honour and Jesus' name.

> "The new way of life brought by the gospel was readily accepted years ago because it was new and exciting. The people thought heaven would come down. But it didn't. The time came when the church seemed to grow lukewarm.
>
> New pastoral upgrading courses are being taught, along with new excitement about women's ministry. We pray God will raise up a spiritually-minded church with leaders who dare to stand up against family and clan pressures."

The questions became more clamorous as Adriaan bared his soul.

> "This is our first full year back, and we do not see much change. When the Ndugas come to see me, the requests are for Community Development projects and flights. Seldom do they come for spiritual counsel. But this is the reason God called us back here, didn't he? This is the question that has crossed my mind more than once and we know he is building his church if we are faithful. He has lots of patience."

He asks the hardest question yet. Is it worth it?

> "We are busy improving our houses, but we have no money to help our preachers to build a decent house for themselves. I continue to ponder the disparity as we live in our comfortable homes while they live in their tiny huts.
>
> Unresponsive young people who would rather paint themselves, grow long hair again, and play hours of volleyball than try to learn to read and write are a burden on our hearts."

This was the state of the church as accurately as Adriaan could express it. The only comfort he could find was that some of his colleagues were struggling with the same questions.

"I know all the arguments for being here. We are here, and we would not want to be anywhere else. God called us back miraculously."

No one had an answer for the questions they all struggled with. Their ranks had been depleted. The tribe was so widespread it was impossible to reach them effectively. They needed more missionary personnel. Everyone seemed busy with their own work. Maybe there were answers. As Adriaan continued to write, the Lord consoled his spirit as he began to remember the ways he had seen God at work.

"I remembered the time when Mijo was walking in the dark. She fell down the stairway, breaking her arm. After waiting a week for the weather to clear so she could fly out and have her arm set in a hospital, Dr. Ken Dresser decided to set the bone remotely. As she prepared to have her bone set, Mijo asked everyone to go down to the airstrip during the procedure. She knew she would scream in pain and didn't want people to hear her. By radio, the doctor instructed two of Elfrieda's medical workers what they needed to do. When Dr. Ken Dresser later checked her arm, the bones were in perfect alignment."

They sensed the support of their colleagues, basking in their friendship and love, expressed in many ways. There were numerous other good things for which to be thankful. Elfrieda observed the gospel's effect when they visited outlying areas.

"Visiting in the peoples' huts, you find pastors studying the Word of God for their Sunday sermons. Sitting in church, it is soul warming to see women with their fingers on the Bible passage the pastor is reading. On some of our helicopter visits to the villages the Ndugas expressed their gratefulness to hear Adriaan's stirring sermons. The Nduga Evangelistic Team returned from long trips, trekking from valley to valley, and church to church, to report on healings and people being revived.

Much prayer had gone up for the people who lived in the Wosak Valley. Pastors were taught to do spiritual warfare where

strongholds of war and killings had occurred and there were encouraging outcomes."

Adriaan was able to visit several areas where no missionary had been
for many years—a tremendous encouragement to the believers in those
churches. The Wosak and Jigi wars have now ended in peace. A good pastoral upgrading course was taught in the Mbuwa for most of the district
pastors. They are now armed with new insights and material to pass on to
their congregations. God through his Spirit is maturing the pastors. Christ
is building a spiritual temple. And he finishes what he begins.

8

CRY OF THE HEART

Since the van der Bijls did not have permanent resident status in the United States, they could not stay out of the country longer than two years. To protect their visa status, they scheduled their mini-furlough to the United States and Europe for June through August 1984. It was significant on several levels. Three of their four children were moving closer to independence and decisions had to be made. Mijo needed to spend time with her mother in Paris. No one could imagine the impact of those visits. Only in hindsight could the family begin to process God's exquisite timing of what would become a pivotal year. When your world turns upside down, it is good to know which way is up. For a while, Adriaan never had the luxury of knowing. It began well enough.

Priorities

When the van der Bijls returned in August, Adriaan addressed one of his concerns. It was about the way the men related to their wives. The women were Mijo's special calling and passion. Her awareness became Adriaan's awareness.

"The work among the women is moving ahead despite some op-
position from the men. The more Mijo works with the women, the
more we realize how lowly a place they have in Nduga society. We
have been appalled many times by the unwillingness of the men to
let their wives take a bigger part in their own lives and that of their
families, not to mention the society and the church. Despite that,
the gospel continues to influence the women, and we pray that it
will spread into the other valleys. To help this process, Mijo and I
traveled into the Mbuwa Valley where we had wonderful meetings
focusing on the women."

More than 300 women attended the meetings. Many rededicated their lives.
Orpa, a God-given women's leader, initiated an early morning prayer meeting for the women.

At the November 2016 Jubilee service in Mapnduma, every service had
a woman emcee and a women's choir. Mary Owen Byrne referred to the impact of Mijo's work: "It was a huge fruit of Mijo's efforts to empower the
women in the Nduga church."

Orit Kwe, another outstanding women's leader, worked alongside her
husband Yulas, a pastor. She is a beautiful woman who loves Jesus with all
her heart. She takes her well-worn Bible and goes from village to village, hut
to hut, to pray for the sick and minister to their needs. She often sees people
healed.

At one of their pastorates, Orit was teaching the women in her literacy
class to read and memorize Scripture. The men already knew how to read,
and the women wanted to learn as well. A lady in her class who had recently
moved in from another valley simply could not learn to read and memorize
Scripture. Her mind was dark and unreceptive.

Orit Kwe asked her, "Lady, is there something on your heart that you
would like to share with me so we can pray about it?"

"Yes," she said, "my husband was a cannibal and would often eat human
flesh. I never did. But one time I was not feeling well, so he gave me some
and I ate it. Then I whistled, and all kinds of noises came out of my mouth.
At dusk, the ghost of the dead person came to haunt me and talked outside
my hut. I know what I did was an awful sin. Please pray for me."

They prayed together and asked God to give her a new heart. The

CRU OF THE HEART

following day she came back a new person. The chains that bound her were gone. She began to memorize and learned to read so quickly. She became a radiant witness for Jesus. Today she worships God with many other women who, liberated from their fear of evil spirits, have found freedom in Christ.

On the home front, the van der Bijl's life at Mapnduma was often on edge, sometimes literally. They were not necessarily safely nestled in their home. After a twelve-hour tropical downpour, part of the mountain behind their house slid down just feet from their home.

> "With roaring power, it took everything in its path, including huge boulders and tree trunks. We had had these landslides before, but every time it seemed to come somewhat closer to our house. When it rains that hard, we always wonder if it will sweep our house away."

The landslide crushed several houses in the Bible School village. Many lost their meager belongings, including several pigs who did not survive.

> "Gardens also slid down into the river, which meant that many would go hungry for some time, but thankfully no lives were lost."

A foretaste of what lay ahead was the visit of three American doctors who were doing advanced research on malaria. Adriaan and Mijo were excited to hear that experimentation was underway on a vaccine for malaria. The doctors said that shortly, the vaccine would be used worldwide which would be a great breakthrough in protection against this vicious killer.

> "An area that needs attention is the hot and muggy Keneyam area, where malaria is rampant. We have found grossly enlarged spleens due to chronic malaria. We look forward to that day when malaria will be under control, and people will live healthier lives."

But how many would have to die before that day would come was a staggering thought. On one of their visits, they were walking down the path when a small boy suddenly fell over. Rushing to his side, they were shocked to find he had died right there on the path. On examination, he showed life-threatening anemia and a grossly enlarged spleen. Malaria together with hookworm infestation was taking a toll on the people's lives.

Other issues were surfacing.

> "Recently an oil company has moved in to start drilling. Of course, this will draw many more people into that area, all wanting to get a piece of the oil cake. With this development, our mountain people will get exposed to malaria, increased cash flow, and other involvements."

Key Events

Adriaan's heart cry never wavered. It reflected David's heart cry in Psalm 61:1 as he reached out to his Father God: Hear my cry, O God; listen to my prayer.

> "The Lord's sustaining grace and love has given us strength to continue behind the ranges. The physical condition of the many valleys that we call the Nduga area will probably never change, but the faithful work of the pastors with the limited knowledge that they have is eternally influencing the Ndugas. We are grateful to the Lord for what is happening and thank him for letting us see a little bit of what it means to have patience and endurance to the end.
>
> One of the pastors reported on the cold reception he had received at his first pastorate from a man who stood and reprimanded him saying, "Who are you to stand up and preach to us?" Two days later this man's house was demolished by a landslide. The young pastor encouraged him to listen to God. He ignored the counsel and while hunting in the forest his son suddenly died. He learned through severe testing and began to attend church and follow God. The grace extended him through this passionate pastor broke his hardened heart.
>
> The last two years our Sion Bible School has been nationalized and run successfully by Nduga teachers with the oversight of a missionary. We praise the Lord for their giftedness and faithfulness and the Spirit's guidance in keeping the school afloat. Some churches are still without a pastor, so prayer is needed for choice

men called by God to come for Bible School training and then return to their villages to teach and disciple the people there."

Adriaan was happy to report that a new District Superintendent was in place with the hope that a new wind might be blowing through the leadership of the Nduga church. He concluded with a prayer: Dear God, may the year ahead be a year of revival and reconciliation, new love and awareness of each other's needs. May Jesus Christ be uplifted. May strong leadership develop. Amen.

"We made a big trip to a new area at Jita, about an hour's flying time south of Mapnduma. A float plane dropped me somewhere on the muddy bank of a river. From there, we had to walk about two hours to where the Ndugas are settling. They carved out a place in the jungle and hoped to build a new village and a brighter future there. An airstrip is possible even though the location is in the marshlands. This will become another outreach point where Ndugas will be taught and discipled in the ways of the Lord. Ministry for Smiley, the local pastor at that time, was not without hardship in this area, but he went, recalling from Matthew 5:12 the words of Jesus: Rejoice and be glad, because great is your reward in heaven, for in the same way they persecuted the prophets who were before you. Smiley knew the world hated Jesus, and this enabled him to serve well. While upholding the high standards of the Lord, his life was threatened at gunpoint by the authorities there. During the storms, he remained faithful though severely persecuted.

I visited the Jigi Valley, along with the local police, to try to settle war issues, but the people are not ready to listen. We were encouraged by the strong and faithful spiritual leadership of Ninsuwon, the District Superintendent in the Jigi. He spoke out against the war, which enraged his relatives. One day as he was on the trail, his relatives lay in ambush for him. They saw him leaving his home alone and thought this would make him an easy target. But when he came closer, they saw a large group of people surrounding him. Confused, they ran away.

Later on, they asked him, "Who were all those people with you?" He replied, "There were no people with me, I was alone." God had sent an army of angels to protect him. The only One who can give victory was his Guardian that day."

The Flourishing Medical Work

Two classes of medical workers were trained and sent to help out in the many far away villages that had churches but no medical help. It is amazing what these medical workers can do with the grass-roots training they have had. The main emphasis is on Bible study and prayer, cleanliness, the building of outhouses, upgrading nutrition with the children under five and, of course, dispensing basic medicines. The goal is to build a small clinic in each of the villages where they will serve, with the help of World Relief Canada. The clinics will benefit the villagers, both physically and spiritually.

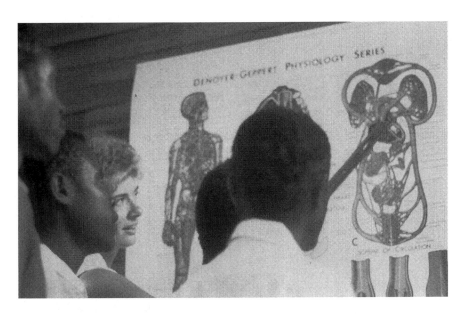

One symptom of protein deficiency shows up in the children's reddish blond hair. A mother brought her five-year-old daughter with severe skin problems and malnutrition to one of the clinics. She returned to her village with a prescription to add seven roasted grasshoppers a day to her breakfast.

Three months later the mother returned and was asked about her little girl's health. "Well, can't you see that this is she?" No one could believe how the grasshopper diet had transformed the emaciated child into a robust little girl with normal black kinky hair.

Kori was the medical worker in the Wosak Valley. He took great delight in upgrading the women and children's health in his village. He encouraged the women to cook sweet potato leaves, add a tablespoon of cooking oil with a pinch of salt and feed it to their children daily. Of course, they also added grasshoppers and other local protein to the children's diet.

Each medical worker had a hang-up scale with weighing pants to weigh the children each month. Kori was diligent with this program and through his contribution observed a significant improvement in the children's health in his village.

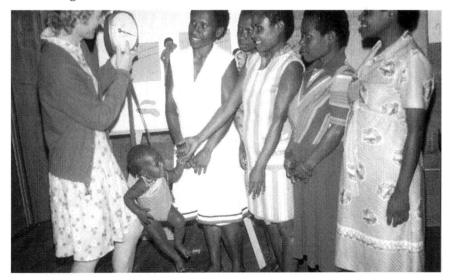

Elfrieda and Staff at Work

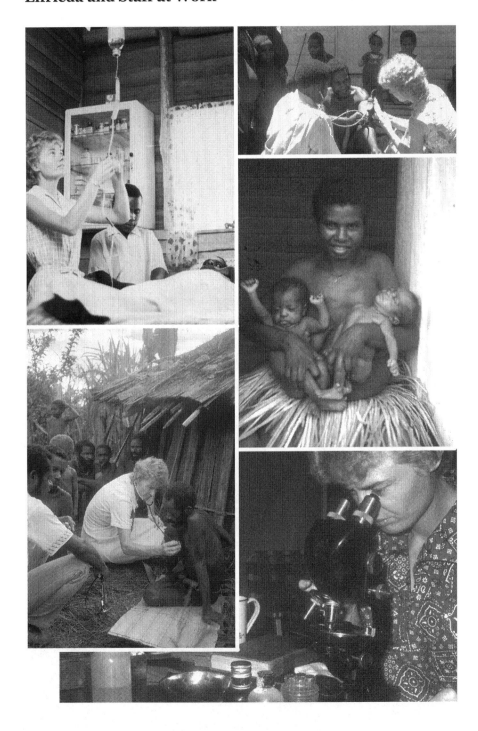

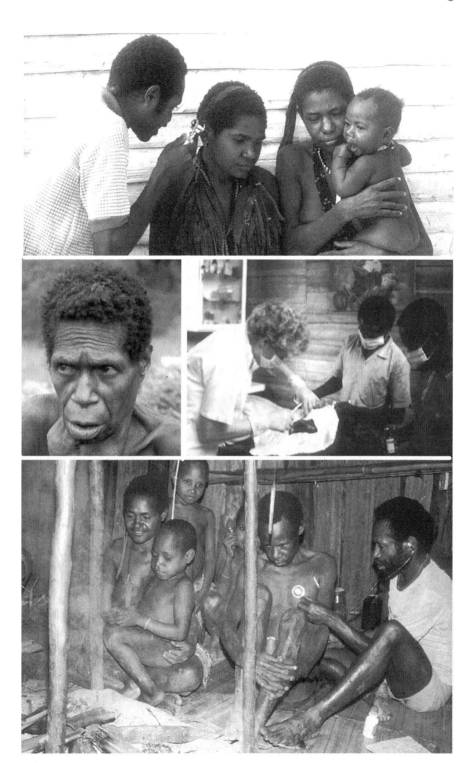

For Adriaan, personal struggles were looming beneath the surface that would rock his world forever. Sometimes all you could do was move, and so Adriaan trudged on the best he could. The road he had chosen was uncertain.

"I took a helicopter into an area that hadn't seen missionaries for many years. I faced heavy swollen rivers, rough trails and an active landslide as I trekked through villages. When I saw their impoverished state, I realized how very little the people in these distant villages had progressed. Arriving just in time for the annual pig feasts, usually held at Christmas, I wondered if these people even knew what it meant. I spent a few days at the church in each village, holding meetings, encouraging them in the Lord and ministering to many physical and spiritual needs."

At the end of the trek, Adriaan and twenty Ndugas attended the opening ceremonies for the Conoco Oil Company, which had set up mining operations at Keneyam. It was a day Adriaan knew was coming and dreaded.

"My heart was heavy, knowing that the materialistic influences of this big American organization would rapidly change the Ndugas' tribal lifestyle."

The Lights Go Out

It is symptomatic of people living in isolated parts of the world that one day blends into another, one year merges into the next. This cryptic journal entry for January 1, 1986 is one of those entries that say more for its brevity than for its festivity. The van der Bijls welcomed the New Year with a New Year's Eve gathering.

"May God give us consistency. We worked on the airstrip. Enjoyed a good New Year's meal with the girls and started to write letters again making plans for 1986."

On Sunday, January 5, Mijo began to feel unwell. Whenever she got sick, her left arm, compromised because of her cancer surgery, was red and painful. She was very uncomfortable that morning when she came downstairs.

Mid-morning, their son Paul called Elfrieda out of children's church because his mother felt so ill.

Elfrieda found that Mijo had malaria-like symptoms. Via radio, she consulted with the mission doctor, Marj Bromley. She asked Elfrieda to take a blood slide for malaria. They then decided what medication to put her on. Mijo began to feel better as the day went on but didn't attend the Sunday evening service in their living room as was her custom.

The next morning Adriaan had a scheduled flight to a business meeting at the coast. Because Mijo appeared to be on the mend, he decided to keep the appointment, trusting her into very good hands.

> "Elfrieda agreed to stay with Mijo even if she seemed to be doing better. I took the blood slide along to the medical clinic in Wamena to be checked out.
>
> Later in the day, I radioed Mapnduma to find out how Mijo was doing. I learned that her right upper arm was so painful that the doctor had prescribed a strong painkiller. Elfrieda was staying overnight at our house to be available if needed."

Adriaan continued his business at the coast while Elfrieda and Paul cared for Mijo, who was in bed most of the time. The blood slide indicated malaria. However, by Wednesday morning, January 8, she was not doing well at all. During the early morning radio call with all the mission stations, Elfrieda asked that Mijo's health issues be included in the prayer chain.

It was a day that Elfrieda has revisited a thousand times since. She had a busy morning scheduled. Nduga parents were bringing their children from the surrounding villages to be weighed and checked at the clinic. She asked Paul to stay with Mijo and to come for her if she was needed.

When Elfrieda arrived to check her at noon, Mijo was sitting on the bed waiting for her. She looked ashen and had a very rapid heart rate. Adriaan has rehearsed the story a thousand times himself. Following is what he pieced together.

> "When Elfrieda checked Mijo's blood pressure, she could not get a reading. With a doctor on the radio, Elfrieda was instructed to start an IV. Mijo's restlessness made Elfrieda wonder if she would

lie still long enough to get an IV running. After Paul put a nail in the ceiling to hold the IV bottle, they prayed for a successful start.

With praise to God, Elfrieda was able to get the IV started on the first attempt. With the IV running, the blood pressure began to respond. Hope rose as her blood pressure increased. But shortly after the second IV, Mijo began to show signs of labored breathing. Elfrieda asked one of the medical assistants to sit back-to-back with her so Mijo could be in a sitting position to help her breathe more easily."

Each time the doctor requested a specific drug via radio Elfrieda had to run across the compound to the clinic to pick up that item and then race back to Mijo's bedside. As she ran back and forth, she encouraged the pastors to gather for prayer. She told them that three pastors at a time could go up to Mijo's room to pray for her. When those three came down, three more could go up. In the flurry of activity, instructions were not followed.

The room gradually filled with Ndugas. In the middle of all the activity and prayer, Yonatan, one of the medical workers who was supporting her arm with the IV saw Mijo raise her head and say, with surprise in her little raspy voice, "Jesus." Then her head dropped down onto her chest.

"By the time Elfrieda came back with the IV Lasix that the doctor had requested, the room was full of people. Mijo's head was down, her body still. Sensing something was wrong, Elfrieda laid her back. Checking her heart, Elfrieda could not hear a sound. It was January 8, 1986 at 5:25 p.m."

Elfrieda went looking for Paul. Finding him, she gently told him that his mother had died. He slumped to the floor in grief. Regaining his composure, he volunteered to tell the doctor via radio.

"Unaware of what had happened in Mapnduma, I waited by the radio for further news about Mijo. Just after 5:30 p.m. I recognized Paul's voice. He simply said, Mom has died. My world went black."

9

SORROWING

WHEN ADRIAAN REGAINED CONSCIOUSNESS, he was lying on a clinic bed with Dr. Ken Dresser close by. Adriaan was in shock. Slowly he attempted to grasp what had happened. It would take months before it could sink in fully. Adriaan writes about the next few days:

> "Mijo and I had agreed that when we died, we wanted to be buried in Irian. We would have to get permission from the governor in Jayapura to be buried in Mapnduma.
>
> However, now my first concern was for our children. I phoned David to tell him of his mother's death. I asked him to call Heidi and Daniel. When I talked to Heidi, I went through the necessary details, although Mijo's death seemed so unreal, even impossible. Heidi immediately decided to come to Irian to help me clean up her mother's stuff. The children expressed their concern for me. I was sustained by God as my colleagues gave expressions of love that evening. I stayed in Jayapura overnight.
>
> Realizing that Mijo would need to be buried the next day, Elfrieda became aware that a funeral would entail a host of

hospitality details—making beds for people to sleep in and having food ready. On the radio she heard Dr. Jerry Powell, Dr. Marj Bromley and me talking about various details of the next day. The question of doing an autopsy came up. Elfrieda said that if I approved, she wanted one done, so she would know what caused Mijo's death. I gave my approval.

The question of where to bury Mijo was raised. I told Elfrieda that I thought the best spot would be a specific grassy knoll near our house. She agreed to make sure a gravesite would be prepared."

Then it started to rain in Mapnduma. As a result, runners couldn't get to other villages to let them know that their beloved missionary, known to them as Ninmin—with us, had died. Everyone was hoping the weather would be better the next day so the runners could spread the word.

"Our house was filled with grieving people throughout the night. When Elfrieda went up to shut off the generator, she stayed to grieve with them awhile. She told them that she wished that she had been the one to die instead of Mijo, a wife and mother, thus causing the breakup of a family. She then went back to her house to make sure that Paul got some sleep even if she couldn't."

Elfrieda reported to Jim Reid, MAF pilot, that the weather was good for flying. In the morning, Dr. Powell flew in at seven a.m. with pilot Dave Rask from Mulia to get the medical history. Jim began to supervise the digging of the grave.

"When Dr. Dresser and I flew in an hour later, Elfrieda met us at the airstrip. Our Field Chairman, John Wilson, joined us. I said that I didn't want to see Mijo's body. Taking me by the hand, John urged me to go with him. We walked to the house, where Ndugas were gathered around her body. They were crying out in their grief, "Why did our mother leave us?"

When I looked at Mijo's face, she seemed to have a slight smile, as if to say, "I surprised you, didn't I?" After I viewed the body, the medical team took her to the clinic to see if they could determine the cause of death. They found plaque in her heart indicating a possible heart attack. Three months later the autopsy results showed that she had died from a fulminating meningococcal infection that led to rapidly evolving severe septic shock."

The pilots prepared some wood planks for the coffin and flew them in when they came from the coast. They assembled the coffin. When the autopsy was complete, Mijo's body was put in the freshly-made casket.

Because the weather was good for flying, MAF was able to arrange five flights into Mapnduma. Several missionaries from other stations, including the Bromleys and the Maxeys, John Hazlett along with AMA pilot Henny, a close Dutch friend, were among the 300 people who gathered for the funeral.

"The service on January 9, 1986, led by John Wilson, was a blend of English and Nduga. Ndugas shared their sorrow for their beloved mother, but the joy she was now experiencing in heaven along with many who had preceded her was rewarding. The Ndugas said, "She was with us in life, bringing us so much blessing. Now she is with us in death." After the service, I led the procession to the gravesite. Some Scriptures were read, and then the coffin was lowered.

Guests, including Lois Bromley and Mark Mungillo, two of Paul's MK friends, gathered at the house for a brief time together. Then MAF started flying the guests out.

Elfrieda declared that she was not going to leave Mapnduma. "How can I leave?" she asked. "How can I desert the Ndugas when their mother has just died? And now we are all going to leave? No way, I'm staying."

Marj Bromley wouldn't hear of it. She arranged for a flight so Elfrieda could leave the next day to recover at the coast for a few days.

When the guests began to leave, I began to cry out, "Mijo, what now?" We had confided and supported each other for more than a quarter century. Who could I talk out the issues and questions with now? Who would keep me grounded when I wanted to rush into a project before it was time?

Life had to continue, so I packed, cleaned and got ready to leave the station. Elfrieda provided a meal for our Field Chairman, John Wilson and his wife, Betty and my son Paul and me that night. I then went back up the hill to my house and crawled into the bed I had shared with Mijo, feeling very much alone.

The next day, January 10, MAF flew in to transport people to their destinations. Elfrieda went with Betty Wilson. I travelled to Wamena to get some business done, then on to Jayapura at the coast. I stayed with Jim and Jean Reid for a few days.

On Saturday, I took a drive by myself. I needed time alone. I cried and cried, sensing the Lord's presence with me. It felt good to be in his hands. "I love you, Lord. What can I do without you?" Finally, I settled enough to spend the evening with our missionary colleagues, the Karceskeys. I phoned Heidi again and gave her more details. I learned that Tutun, Mijo's sister, had left for Paris. I was grateful, since I didn't have contact information and couldn't phone Mijo's mother to tell her that her beloved daughter had died.

The next few days, I kept busy. On Wednesday, January 15, I registered Mijo's death with the government. That day we had a very meaningful memorial service with the missionaries at Sentani, including our colleague, Mary Owen, who had now returned from being with her mother in the United States.

The grieving process was so new to me. I wondered what the future would hold. I was reassured that the Lord would lead. He had been so wonderful. It was so different to be alone. I would ask Mijo what to do but I heard no reply. In the silence, I turned to God, told him I loved him and asked that he settle me down."

What Now?

Adriaan decided that it would be helpful to take a boat trip with Paul. The day after the memorial service, they boarded the cruise ship *Umsini* at Jayapura for a ten-day cruise. Following the cruise, Paul resumed his studies at Penang, Malaysia. Adriaan met Heidi at Jakarta January 23; they flew to Mapnduma together.

Back in Mapnduma, Elfrieda was working through her own understanding of what life might be like without her beloved colleague. Mary Owen was staying with Elfrieda, even though she had been appointed secretary to our Field Chairman at Jayapura. When Elfrieda prepared to return to Mapnduma, she realized that she just could not go back alone. She needed someone to go with her for emotional support. The return was too difficult to handle alone. Mijo's death was such a sudden and painful passing. Each time Elfrieda reviewed the events of Mijo's death, she went over again and again what might have been and how she could have done things differently.

News of Mijo's death and burial was beginning to spread. Runners had left to tell the other villages as soon as the rain had stopped. However, the people were angry because they had not been notified in time to attend the service in Mapnduma. In grief and anger, the Ndugas in one village threatened to wipe Mapnduma off the map. Fortunately, they didn't carry out their threats. By the time Adriaan and Heidi arrived, the threats had evaporated. The Ndugas surrounded Adriaan and Heidi as they grieved together at Mijo's gravesite. Heidi was a big help to her dad as they were going through her mother's things.

"The house seemed empty without Mijo's happy chatter. It was a bittersweet time for the two of us. Mary and Elfrieda provided our main meal each day so that we were free to sort through Mijo's personal things and determine what to do with them."

Even during his personal grief, Adriaan was called on to settle rumblings of war. War going on in the Jigi would not wait for him to process his own loss.

> "Heidi flew with me to the Jigi. Then I needed to go to the Mbuwa. Heidi went there with me. Her time with me was special and much too short. She flew back to the United States on February 17, 1986."

By this time, Mary had to leave to resume her secretarial duties. Mission field policy did not allow Adriaan to stay alone with Elfrieda on the station. The policy at that time, and in those isolated circumstances, was clear. There was no way around it. Two single missionaries of the opposite sex were not allowed to live on the same mission station. Elfrieda was there alone. As Educational Coordinator, Adriaan went to Pyramid to evaluate the Bible School there.

Meanwhile, MAF had determined that the airstrip at Mapnduma should be repaired. They realized that Adriaan would not be there much longer, so they requested that the repairs be done immediately.

> "Since I wasn't at Mapnduma when I got the notice, I radioed Elfrieda. I asked her to have people bring sand and whatever else was needed to get the airstrip upgraded. When I came back to Mapnduma to do the upgrade, we found ourselves in an uncomfortable situation because of the mission's policy and the closure of the airstrip.

I worked on the airstrip until it was ready to be reopened in April. I also worked on Mijo's gravesite, cemented it in and made a plaque with her Nduga name, Ninmin on it. The people were pleased, believing she would be with them for all time."

With the airstrip closed, Elfrieda and Adriaan had to learn how to interact with each other. It may have been a timely conversation that would never have happened if the airstrip had not needed repair. But it was still uncomfortable knowing that the circumstances had thrown them together in contravention of the conduct they understood to be accepted practice.

"We made sure that other people were always there when we were in the same house. However, there was more that needed to be worked through."

Elfrieda remembers that she had wondered how she should relate to him. She concluded that she should treat him like a brother. So, as a sister, she prepared meals for them at her house.

Adriaan stayed busy outside, doing a lot of work on the airstrip. They only came together for meals. They always made sure the houseboy was there so there wouldn't be rumours. The tension was relieved when Adriaan travelled to Keneyam or went out with the oil company by helicopter as needed.

Matchmaker

By May 1, 1986 the airstrip was permitted to open, and the immediate awkwardness diminished. A big Nduga Church Conference and retreat at Mapnduma was scheduled for that month, and Adriaan looked forward to friends coming in. The pilot, Jim Reid and his wife, Jean, also flew in and the awkwardness ramped up.

"Jean Reid came over to chat with me. As we talked, she began to ask some searching questions. What I was thinking? What did I think the future might look like? Would I go back to Holland and stay there? Might I come back again? She continued to probe, asking me if I had thought of asking Elfrieda to be my wife?"

Adriaan mustered the only stunning response that came to mind, "I don't know yet." It was a telling response even though Mijo's death was still a gaping wound. In his mind, he was thinking that it was too soon—only five months after the death of his wife. It seemed too early to be talking about getting married again. Besides, remarriage would probably be upsetting for his children.

> "Jean continued to probe, asking me who I would choose if I were to consider remarriage. She was putting me on the spot. I decided to reply honestly and told her Elfrieda would be my first choice. The Lord had already kind of spoken to me about Elfrieda."

Then Jean Reid went down to visit Elfrieda at her home. As they were reminiscing, Elfrieda mentioned how much she missed Mijo. Jean piped up, "Oh I was just up there talking to Adriaan, and he said you were his first choice should he remarry." Elfrieda was stunned. Jean demanded an answer, so after some thought Elfrieda said, "Why don't you tell him we can talk about it." Jean did not seem satisfied with that evasive answer.

Later Elfrieda pondered, "If only my sister Elsie were here to talk about this." She was all alone. What would she do? She was on the spot. It was a big decision to make by herself. Then the Lord responded, "You can ask me. I will tell you." She committed it to the Lord. He gave her a peace in her heart that she found hard to believe.

Adriaan enjoyed the fellowship with colleagues during the Nduga Church Conference. When everyone returned to their home base, he was again alone with his thoughts. He was scheduled to fly out to the coast May 14, then on to Holland and Europe.

He was very aware that in a few days he would be leaving for Holland.

10

STRAND OF THREE

THE DAY AFTER ADRIAAN PROPOSED to Elfrieda the plane came bright and early. It dropped off some cargo and then flew on to Akimuga. It would return an hour later to take Mary and Adriaan out.

> "After the three of us checked the inventory unloaded from the plane, I asked Elfrieda, "Why don't you come up to the house and I will inform you about the fridge and freezer and stuff." While we were at my house, I gave her a kiss and a hug. Soon the plane returned. Mary and I climbed aboard leaving Elfrieda alone in Mapnduma.
>
> When I saw Jim and Jean Reid, I told them about our plans. Jean, the matchmaker, was elated. I also talked to John Wilson, the Field Chairman, asking him to announce our engagement at the C&MA Field Conference in July. I asked everyone to keep the news secret."

Adriaan picked up Paul who was at the MK school in Penang, Malaysia. Together they headed to Europe and a visit with Mijo's mom.

"Mijo had been her special daughter. As we chatted, she told me when we said goodbye to her several years ago, that she sensed she would not see Mijo again. When I told her that I would probably get married, she interrupted to suggest that the nurse who helped Mijo in her last hours would be a good choice. Amazing!

Meanwhile, the news was beginning to leak out. When she heard this, Elfrieda asked that the team leader make the announcement as early in the program at the Field Conference as possible. When John Wilson said that he had a very interesting announcement to make, everyone was in suspense. They all cheered as he announced the engagement.

"When the long-awaited audio tape from missionary friends in Irian arrived. I went to my car to listen to it. It was so good to hear their voices and their reactions to our engagement. I could not have a more supportive missionary family. We have peace about this new adventure that only the Lord can give, and we want to give him the glory for the life he is leading us to share together.

The verses in Psalm 30:11, 12 were such a reality to me after Mijo's homegoing: You have turned my mourning into dancing; you have loosed my sackcloth and girded me with gladness. This promise has become more significant in the light of the latest developments. Rejoice with us."

For Adriaan, the respite from Irian Jaya, coupled with the chance to process his grief with family was a special gift.

"For me, they were days of happiness because I had the whole family together. My children accepted the news of my engagement to Elfrieda, a real answer to prayer. Their relationship with her will be different, but I believe it will be meaningful."

More Engagement Cheers

In Mapnduma, Elfrieda was steeling herself for the most significant transition of her life. The shift from a colleague to the wife was daunting enough but becoming the wife of your best friend's husband would test her mettle. Moving from colleague to marriage partner, sharing the same work environment, and navigating the same cultural and labour dynamics would take time to figure out. It was time to lay new tracks, and as with all she tackled in life, she took this transition in stride as well. She took the time to collect her thoughts and communicate her sentiments with her team family before she left Mapnduma to marry Adriaan. As Elfrieda brought this chapter to a close, there was a sense that she did not know what was ahead precisely. She knew she needed to take time to bring closure to the single chapter of her life. To some extent, it was scary. Her routine would change dramatically. There was a lot they did not know about each other. She was closing the door on twenty years of history. She had no way to anticipate what that next chapter might hold.

> "Thank you for the many kindnesses you, as our mission family, have shown me in innumerable and caring ways—the pilots bringing in special mail bags, those who gave helpful radio advice, who wrote special notes, the delightful shower and especially to Jim and Dee Sunda who have so capably taken over the Mapnduma responsibilities—to mention just a few."

Elfrieda noted the reaction of the Nduga people to the news. The announcement had been passed on to them via radio. At Mapnduma, Nduga District Superintendent Sakius Lokmbere announced it in church on Sunday. At Keneyam, Simon Dimiye excitedly blew his bamboo horn and brought the whole village running to see what had happened. In both places, they broke into spontaneous applause with a joyous wiwa-o when they heard that Ndugamende—Adriaan was planning to marry Nduga kwe—Elfrieda.

The medical worker's reaction was somewhat reserved until Elfrieda assured them that she would continue her medical ministry with them.

Elfrieda noted the number of people who had been concerned about her when they learned of Mijo's death. They realized her need for a partner to help with the work at Mapnduma. People had been praying that she would get a special partner to help her.

> "I am amazed as I see how God's plan has developed. We praise the Lord for the beautiful mission family we have in Irian Jaya standing with us through thick and thin. There is no other place

in the world where the family of God shows more warmth, care, concern, and genuine love. We feel so honoured by your love for us. What a heritage!"

Elfrieda kept Adriaan abreast of wedding developments. She had written home and asked her sisters to schedule the wedding for December 27, 1986. Elsie and Elviera would be part of the wedding planning strategy.

First on their list was a lunch with Pastor Walter Boldt, pastor of Circle Drive Alliance in Saskatoon, their home church. When the pastor returned, he told the staff that there would be a mystery wedding on December 27th.

The next day Millie Miners, a church member who had been praying for someone to help Elfrieda at Mapnduma, was visiting Elsie and Elviera and asked about the situation. The secret was out!

The wedding was no longer a mystery.

Wedding Bells and Blaring Sirens

Wedding plans began in full flurry. Elfrieda arrived home from Irian in October. Typical of a make-do farm girl, she found her dream wedding dress for ninety-nine dollars. A good friend added her sewing expertise and out came the perfect fit with brocade embellishment and a flowing veil.

Elfrieda wanted an international flavor. Lenna Anderson, a Papuan teenager, nurtured and later adopted by Irian Jaya missionaries, was one of her bridesmaids. They wore kebayas in shades of burgundy and pink, a blouse and skirt combination typically worn by Indonesian women. Eko Pinardi, an Indonesian pilot, studying with MAF in Chicago, was an usher.

"Our wedding was special with many friends and family together
with us. Having my children with me for another day after the
wedding extended the happiness."

Starting off on their honeymoon, the newlyweds drove across the border into the United States at a remote crossing. In the excitement of the
moment and in the blush of being newlyweds they failed to recognize the
border crossing or hear the blaring sirens. They drove on in marital bliss for
a few miles!

"The border guards didn't believe that we did not hear their sirens.
They hauled us back to the border and told us they could take our
car away and fine us $5,000. The guards were not impressed with
our apologies."

The officials wanted to know more about this strange story and this odd couple in the car. There was nothing Adriaan and Elfrieda could do but tell them

about a far-away place called Mapnduma. The explanation seemed so far-fetched that it could not have been anything other than true. Missionaries tend to make poor liars. The border guards finally accepted the statement and let them go.

> "We drove to Atlanta, Georgia in the cold of a January month.
> Then on to the warmth of Puerto Rico for our honeymoon."

The warmth of new love, rekindled companionship, and fresh discovery of each other made Mapnduma seem like a distant memory.

The New Normal

After a 1987 winter missions tour in frigid western Canada, the couple was soon back in Irian Jaya. Everything including their wedding and honeymoon faded into the background.

It must have been strange for Adriaan to return to Mapnduma with his new wife. There was no Mijo to greet him this time. They were living in the house Elfrieda and Mary had lived in for years. For Elfrieda, it must have been equally strange not to greet her faithful colleague, Mijo, but to return as Adriaan's wife. Whatever the emotions, there was no time for reflection.

Both Adriaan and Elfrieda picked up where they had left off. Adriaan was Coordinator for Theological Education, and Elfrieda continued as the Nduga Coordinator for the C&MA Medical Services. They both travelled extensively, usually at the same time but in different directions. Adriaan was in constant committee meetings which took him to Jakarta and Yogyakarta in Java and most of the Bible Schools in Irian Jaya. Elfrieda travelled to dispense medicines at Pyramid for all the C&MA mission stations in Irian Jaya. She set up several new clinics in the outlying Nduga areas, with World Relief assistance. She was also involved in several training seminars for the medical workers at Pyramid and Silimo.

Airstrip construction and women's ministry filled in the rest of their days. There was no end to requests for more airstrips to make their isolated valleys more accessible. Adriaan also needed to supervise repairs at other airstrips, taking advantage of the helicopter's presence in their valleys to visit and encourage the people as well.

In a sort of sidebar, as the ministry grew in the Mbuwa, Adriaan participated in a baptismal service of ninety people and in the communion service
that followed. For some missionaries, that would have been a career's work.
He was encouraged that the people were eager to listen to God's Word and
obediently follow the Lord in baptism.

> "I could see that using the helicopter rather than trekking would
> be the primary mode of transportation to the remote valleys in
> the future. I was also asked to build more bridges. The rattan
> swinging bridges rot so quickly. By using steel rods instead of the
> rattan, these bridges would continue to be a lifeline for the people
> travelling the trails."

There were two more airstrips to service, and the only way to get to them
was hitting the trail again. Adriaan loved being on the trail. Out there in
the open, he could fellowship with God and the Ndugas in a closer way. He
enjoyed the beauty and peace of God in the rainforest and the friendship
of those he trekked with on these long trips. Adriaan's willingness to walk
where they walked made him like a brother to them which they highly treasure to this day. He always received a warm welcome in each village, visibly
evident by the pig feast they lavished on him.

Celebrating With a Pig Feast

Adriaan and Elfrieda had seen the ritual pig feast a hundred times. It's an event like no other. Pigs own the place. To make a finger-licking pig feast, you need both sweet potatoes and pork. The pork and sweet potatoes are steamed in pits in the ground using hot rocks.

The pits are lined with leaves, into which the sweet potatoes are layered and interspersed with sweet potato leaves.

Trees are chopped down and cut into pieces of wood to heat the rocks. The logs are stacked up with the stones piled on top. The rocks become so hot that they are wrapped in banana leaves, so the sweet potatoes don't burn.

Then comes the pig. The pig is placed on top of the pit full of sweet potatoes and greens, hide side facing up.

The rocks help to build up steam in the pit. The pit is closed tightly with the leaves that lined the pit and extra rocks and earth placed on top for a pressure-cooker-tight result.

While the food cooked, everyone gathered for a worship service as Adriaan shared the life-transforming gospel with them.

By then the aroma from the pits was wafting into the air, and people were eager to open them and distribute the food. Soon everyone was seated enjoying the mouth-watering meal together.

Constant Concern for Total Well-Being

Adriaan's vision to focus on secular education for the Nduga young people demonstrated his constant concern for the total well-being of the Ndugas, not just the spiritual dimension of his calling. Latecomers who saw the foreigners as soul savers and negative cultural change agents who damaged the culture and left little in return would have little ground to stand on.

> "We had Nduga teachers and nurses but would like to see other professionals trained: government officials, mayors, lawyers, doctors, pilots and other professionals. With Nduga young people now trained in universities, this was already taking place."

Adriaan decided they could not stretch themselves thin enough. Though he was grateful for what they had already accomplished throughout twenty-five years in Nduga country with the Bible School and upgrading seminars for pastors, he yearned for a deeper knowledge of God in their lives, before their time ran out. He was not blind to the reality that their time in Nduga country might be ending.

Things were not going as smoothly with the women's work. Leaders were jealously clinging to their positions and prestige. They did not want Elfrieda's helper, Meme, to lead them, despite her godly leadership skills, because they wanted to keep their old positions.

What was new to Elfrieda was that she now had Adriaan to support her in the squabbles and process the disagreements. Being able to talk things through with the ladies and give input was helpful and bolstered her credibility with the women. Adriaan took over the financial responsibility and tracking of medical supplies. It lifted a huge load from her shoulders. They were learning to work as a team.

Personal Losses

Woven into the fabric of daily living was the constant thread of losses, large and small. On December 7, 1987, they received word from Canada that the husband of Elfrieda's sister, Anna, had been killed when he was hit by a car.

> "The Nduga women immediately broke down, crying and praying with us. They live so close to death, understand its pain and weep with those who weep."

Amid their struggle for survival, the Nduga people were quick to recognize and respond to the losses of others. Adriaan and Elfrieda always experienced the warmth of their Nduga family in times of crisis.

One afternoon, a torrential rainstorm let loose.

> "The seven-year-old son of a couple attending the Sion Bible School convinced his five-year-old sister to watch the water flowing in a stream bed right behind their hut. He held a little door over his head to keep the rain off himself while his sister used a small piece of aluminum. As they clambered to a spot where they

could watch the rushing water, a landslide developed. It took everything in its path, gathering up trees and mud and sweeping up the two children as it thundered down the mountainside. After several hours, the searchers saw little toes sticking out from under the debris and uncovered the two bodies lying side-by-side, unscarred but dead."

In an act of compassion, Adriaan and Elfrieda arranged a helicopter to take the mother and the bodies to their village home. Their father, a pastor, had trekked to his home village to minister several days before the disaster.

The people in the village of Koroptak were very superstitious and were going to blame the deaths on witches. The father stood his ground and declared, "You must not talk about witchcraft. The Lord gave me these children, and he has taken them away. Blessed be the name of the Lord. I still have two." He dedicated one of the two remaining children to Christ the next Sunday, December 27, 1987 saying, "God gave them to me. They are not mine. I give them back to God."

Mourning, again

Elfrieda listened to join the Prayer and Praise reports on the radio, as part of her normal routine. When it was over, her colleague Edith Hansen asked her to change to channel three for a private conversation. Elfrieda wrote:

"She told me that she had just taken a phone call from Elsie to tell me that our little mother had peacefully passed into the Lord's presence. I was alone when I received the message and immediately began to weep."

The news spread. About thirty to forty women came into the living room to mourn with Elfrieda. They cried, prayed and sang:

Heaven is a place with no more crying, ye-e wo-o, ye-e, wo-a.
No sickness and no more death, ye-e, wo-o.
There will only be eternal joy, ye-e, wo-o.

The room was filled with worship, prayer and praise to God for a widowed mother who unselfishly gave her daughters to bring the gospel to Irian. Then they sent a message to Anna, Elsie, Elviera, and family.

"Your mother gave us her children unselfishly because of Jesus' command to go to the ends of the earth with the gospel. All these years she prayed for us so faithfully. Now we mourn because she left us. But we rejoice that she has gone to be with her Saviour. Thank you, a thousand times."

Elfrieda was moved when even the men came to weep and weep and weep. Several missionaries encouraged her over the radio and Adriaan also came on the radio to comfort her. She spent the rest of the day reflecting on what her mother had meant to her.

"I cannot begin to thank the Lord for her life. Her influence and willingness to let my sisters Elsie and Elviera and I go to the mission field, though she was a widow, and to stand so supportively behind us here is precious."

The confirmation of God's purposes in their lives through supernatural revelation helped them make sense of the losses or at least, mediate the loss. Up until now, the loss of Mijo had been a deep personal loss that Elfrieda had experienced. But the loss of her mother was a deeper blow. The losses kept coming and there was nowhere to look but up.

Elfrieda remembered that the Lord spoke to her midwife, Dorti, through dreams many times. When Dorti's mother died, the Lord comforted her through a dream. The night Elfrieda's mother passed away Dorti had been working with the delivery of a premature baby off and on. After Dorti went home to sleep, she had a dream. In it, someone told her that Elfrieda's mother had gone home to heaven. The next morning, she learned that Elfrieda's mother had died.

In the sadness, some strands of three seemed somehow to have weathered the storm. The strand of three sisters was still intact, though stretched by loss and distance. The strand of Adriaan, Mijo and Elfrieda seemed somehow to have survived despite her parting. And the strand of three that was strongest, Elfrieda's love for Adriaan, her mother, and the Nduga people was forever cemented.

11

A MINDSET FOR MISSIONS

FOR ELFRIEDA, THE INFLUENCES toward a mission mindset began at an early age.

> "The children's hour stories on Saturday evenings via radio made a real impact on our young minds. With no television or videos, books enlarged our world and shaped our future. Mother was an avid reader and would gather us around her as she read many moving missionary stories to us."

When a classmate asked Elfrieda and Elviera what they planned to do when they grew up, they both said, "We're going to be missionaries."

> "That desire and passion never left us. The biography of David Livingston, missionary to Africa, also marked my life for missions. When I was ten, a Canadian Sunday School Mission volunteer came to our farm inviting us to a Bible camp. Money was scarce, but if

we memorized 200 Bible verses, we could go for free. Those verses remain embedded in our hearts. Summer camp became a real highlight especially because there we met real live missionaries."

Farm life was good missionary training. Being responsible for farm chores, running machinery, and driving trucks all taught coping skills. On a remote station, Elfrieda adapted that expertise to survive on her own, as she became adept at developing a wide variety of skills. She was comfortable building shelves for a clinic, getting advice via radio on fixing her generator, and even butchering a cow that did not make it through a delivery (together with her sister Elsie and lots of Nduga help).

To get an education in a rural setting Elfrieda took her first two years of high school by correspondence, her third year in a Christian boarding school, and her final year in a public collegiate. Then it was off to nurse's training. It had been her childhood dream, but little did she realize what that training would prepare her to do.

"I fondly remember the first delivery I witnessed which was an exhilarating experience. Emergency room experience introduced me to witnessing my first suture case, where I almost passed out, but it opened my world to scores of opportunities to use my skills in suturing up wounds on my future jungle station."

The sudden passing of her father left a huge void in the family, but he had prepared his children well. After nurse's training Elfrieda headed off with her two sisters to the Canadian Bible College in Regina, Saskatchewan. The heritage of godly parents was pointing her squarely toward her destiny.

Three Sisters

For young people who were candidates for foreign mission careers in the 1960's, the C&MA leadership made it clear that they did not place family members in the same country. The policy meant that the three sisters, Elsie, Elfrieda, and Elviera, who had all made application for foreign mission service, could not expect to be assigned to the same field. They had always made decisions together. Well aware that they may not see each other for years at a time, there was no turning back. Their dependence was on the Lord.

Elfrieda, Elviera, Elsie

There was another matter. Whether in the heat of eagerness to present the applications to the mission sending body or not, the sisters had forgotten or failed to keep their mother in the loop. Perhaps they thought that they would submit their applications first and tell mother later. It may reflect a lack of confidence that the C&MA would even consider prairie girls for what they felt was a noble and high calling.

When Elfrieda's mother read the letter that said her daughters were making application for overseas missionary service, she was stunned. The girls went home to Saskatoon to explain more fully to their mother who slowly began to embrace the idea that her daughters were destined for the nations. And perhaps there was a chance they would not be accepted.

"It was late on a Saturday afternoon. Our sister Elsie received an airmail letter from C&MA Headquarters informing her that she was accepted for service and was to be in Irian Jaya (formerly the island of Dutch New Guinea) by May 1. We looked at a large world map to find the place. Wow—were we excited! But I knew then I would not be going there.

Two days later, on Monday I had laryngitis and was in my dorm room. My sisters were in class when Elviera saw the mailman go by the door and put an airmail envelope into our mailbox. She slipped out, saw my name on it, and rushed to my room with it. It looked identical to Elsie's. I ripped it open. Elfrieda Toews is appointed to West Irian to be there by May 1, 1963. Wait a minute! That's a duplicate of Elsie's letter! But no—it had my name on it. My laryngitis vanished! I rushed from room to room to announce the good news. Soon the college was abuzz with the news flash— the Toews sisters to be in Irian Jaya before May 1."

Elfrieda and Elsie left their Saskatoon home March 30. The landing at Sentani Airport with its beautiful palm trees blowing in the breeze gave them a glimpse of a country that was already dear to their hearts. It was a gorgeous place with breathtaking scenery, trees in bloom everywhere. And their first introduction to banana trees.

They settled in. Elsie began teaching at the Sentani MK school as soon as she arrived. Elfrieda was helping Edith Hansen and Vonnie Heiden in the C&MA office in the capital city of Jayapura, along with learning some Indonesian, until the Field leadership decided where her medical skills were needed.

Elviera was not with them. It would be three years before they would be together in their adoptive land. The political situation in Irian Jaya was such that it would be a long wait before Elviera's visa was granted. When the call from the C&MA headquarters in New York finally came in September 1966 to say that her visa had come through, Elviera quickly packed up and flew the same route to join her sisters. She would be teaching at the same MK school as Elsie. When she arrived Elsie and her entire class of grades five to eight students were waiting to welcome her to Irian Jaya.

My People, South of the Ranges

Elfrieda's call to the Nduga people intersects with Adriaan's at this point because God was building a team and what God had in mind for the Nduga

people could only be accomplished through someone with medical training. When Elfrieda first heard of the Nduga people something resonated
instantly.

"When I heard their story, my heart pounded, and excitement
rose. Instantly I knew these were my people. I had always wanted
a challenging medical work in a tribe of people who had never
heard of Jesus. I began to share my desire and determination with
various missionaries. But would I be allowed to go? I was single.
They needed a male missionary to walk in to build an airstrip for
the plane to land.

It was the month of May 1963. I would have to wait till
mid-July when our appointments came up for discussion at our
annual Field Conference at Pyramid. As the weeks rolled by, my
anticipation grew. Finally, the day arrived. Elsie and I left the pic-
turesque north coast as we boarded a MAF plane at the Sentani
Airport. On our way to Pyramid, we looked down on an endless
stretch of dense jungle. Soon the mountains appeared and then
a distinct pyramid-shaped mountain came into view. It must be
Pyramid mission station.

The people looked just like we had seen them on the many
slides that the Irian Jaya missionaries had shown us at Canadian
Bible College. We had arrived at last. These were my people. More
anxious days awaited me. It seemed like I was called in every day
to be interviewed by the Allocations Committee and had no idea
of the outcome. I kept praying. It was the last day, and still no
answer. Saturday afternoon just before the evening meal I was
called in. They told me to sit down and proceeded to pray. Then
the chairman of the committee read my allocation. Elfrieda Toews
is appointed to the Nduga tribe.

Really? Had I heard right? Yes! I controlled my excitement
until I got out of the office. I dashed to the dining room to tell
my friends. I was going to work with the Nduga tribe. God had
answered my prayers. He had counted me worthy. He had raised
up a team of four: Adriaan and Mijo van der Bijl, the trailblazer
and strip builder, along with Mary Owen, the linguist. Mary had

worked in the Ilaga for five years and was fluent in Damal so could use two bilingual Damal/Nduga informants to begin reducing the Nduga language to writing. Elfrieda Toews would complete the team as a nurse. And so began the story of the opening of God's work among the Nduga tribespeople. I praised and thanked God over and over for his goodness in selecting me to live among and serve the Nduga people.

The launch of a lifetime ministry for me was thrilling. With my nurse's training and Bible College completed, God had now granted me the desire of my heart. A people begging for a missionary to model the gospel message to this extraordinary tribe. An opportunity. An open door."

A Brand-New World

The prairie girl went on to make a momentous mark among the Nduga people. She was more than up to the challenge. What she accomplished in that world is legendary among the Nduga people. From a single clinic in Mapnduma during her first term, her ministry extended throughout the mountainous valleys, of which Mapnduma is the center. When she retired to the Canadian prairie in 1998, thirty-five clinics dotted the landscape of Ndugaland, staffed by eighty Nduga medical workers she had trained and deployed to reach out into their little villages where the needs were greatest. Midwives had been trained and were available to assist the women in pregnancy and childbirth.

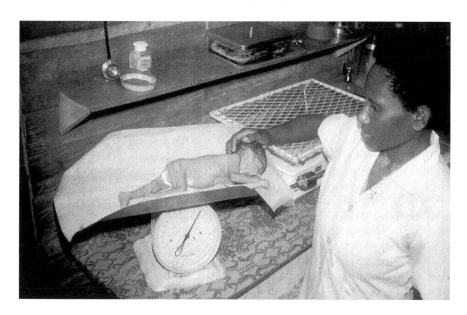

Women now have a new place in Nduga society. Mijo, Mary, and Elfrieda dared to move into a male-dominated culture and push back against the traditions and superstitions that had bound women in subjection and abuse. Elfrieda never hesitated to take on the impossible and propel it into reality.

Preparing to Serve

The genius of Elfrieda's work was her ability to recruit and train Nduga medical workers. She was patient, yet demanding and firm. Diligent in explaining the most elementary concepts to young people born into a Stone Age culture, Elfrieda's teaching was totally unlike training in a North American setting. Her students were bright, yet in their culture, they seldom knew how old they were. They determined that by how old someone was who was born at the same time. It helped them figure it out when they lost their two front teeth. Or perhaps they become aware of their age when they become interested in someone of the opposite sex. They needed to learn how to read a thermometer. The importance of boiling syringes after every use took firm reminders day after day. Elfrieda persevered, providing constant refresher courses and upgrading when trainees were ready. Before graduation each medical worker was required to fill out a form with the following questions.

> Will you be willing to put your patients first?
>> Even if you are hungry,
>> if it is raining,
>> if they come in the middle of the night,
>> if it is your enemy,
>> if you are tired?
> Will you do it all for the Lord?

"As I looked over the sixth-grade primary school grads, I spotted a young graduate who was always smiling. I knew Dinus was a suitable prospect for the medical program.

When I asked him if he would consider this ministry, he responded favourably. A top-notch student, he was a dynamic asset to the medical team. Dinus' affirmative response to the questions that were one of my requirements is still his mandate twenty-five years later. He continues to say that on his forehead these words are written: I don't do it unto man but unto the Lord. When patients come to Dinus, they are all equal, and all receive the same treatment. He expects nothing in return."

Three Ndugaland Case Studies

Hundreds of case stories and treatments and losses will never be known, but a few stories that Elfrieda recorded will provide a sampling of her ministry.

"We were reading in bed, taking time to unwind from a busy day. There was a loud knock on our door. A loud, shrill voice informed us, "Moneka just had her baby, but the placenta has not delivered! She is dizzy. Come quickly." I grabbed my medical bag and solar light and hurried about ten minutes up the hill. As we reached Moneka, we saw a group huddled around a little kerosene lamp in the yard behind the hut. Moneka's husband, medical worker

Sepianus, was supporting her. I investigated, and indeed the placenta was firmly inside. As we prayed, God did a miracle. Along with the Psalmist in Psalm 77:14, we applauded the God who performs miracles; who displays his power among the peoples as the placenta slipped out."

Adriaan and Elfrieda had invited MAF pilot, David Marfleet and his family for Easter weekend. They had just finished eating when the Ndugas arrived asking for help. Ap Misik was injured while working high up in a pandanus nut tree. He was working while perched on two branches when one of the branches broke. He fell, breaking his lower leg in half. He forced the bone back together by himself. Several people tried to get him down the steep mountain slope. With a swollen broken lower leg, they couldn't bring him down piggyback. A stretcher was out of the question because of the slope.

David told them to clear a forty-foot section of the forest. In the morning, they were to light a fire so he could guide a helicopter to the area. The next morning, pilot Marfleet landed on the newly constructed landing pad. It was a godsend to have everything available in God's perfect timing.

The Nduga church service that Easter was enriched with David preaching and singing Indonesian songs accompanied by their girls on their guitars. After a lovely chicken dinner with steamed pudding for dessert, they had a relaxing afternoon together. In the evening after the children were in bed, they had a most blessed time of sharing. For them, the weekend was a spiritually uplifting and enriching time of sharing, refuelling, and rededication to the Lord for the days ahead.

Elfrieda was teaching in her clinic classroom when she heard a cry for help. The student medical workers ran out and yelled that an earthslide had buried someone. Elfrieda ran outside. The front yard of her home was surrounded by scores of people, digging frantically with shovels and garden digging sticks to reach the victim.

A few ladies had been gathering clay from a knoll to repair the surface of the Mapnduma airstrip. They dug four feet into the bottom of an incline creating a cavity with about three feet of earth above them. One lady had left, another was on her way out, carrying their loads of clay in gunny sacks to the airstrip. Wandikmbi was still digging out more clay, likely on her knees, when the ground collapsed, burying her. The clay was too heavy for her to shove aside and escape. She was a sweet lady, whose husband, a Bible School graduate, had died four months earlier. Our hearts sank.

> "It took at least ten minutes for dozens of people, digging frantically with shovels and garden digging sticks to locate her body. When I arrived, she was still breathing. However, she was in a deep coma, with wounds on her head, a possible broken neck, shoulder blade, and leg. We cleaned her mouth and suctioned her for mucous. Her heartbeat was slow and waning. Soon there was no pulse and no blood pressure. It was a heartbreaking time for us, her daughter, and extended family members. For her, nothing in all of heaven could begin to compare with meeting Jesus face to face."

House Calls

A house call, Nduga style, was different than grabbing your medical kit and heading for the car. It involved climbing into a small plane or a helicopter, and corkscrewing through twisty mountain passes and landing on a dime.

> "The first stop for Adriaan and me was the Kora Valley. The plan was to land the helicopter at the clinic, but the people were already at the airstrip site. We airdropped the medical supplies

there without landing and flew twenty minutes south to the muggy lowlands where sweat poured down as if we had stepped into a steam room. The women at Keneyam hugged us, the men shook hands, and the kids were so excited to see us. The people there were extremely anemic with grossly enlarged spleens, indicating that hookworm and malaria are real killers. We took time to examine those who needed care and to instruct the medical workers in proper treatment. The Ndugas were so grateful for our visit that they showered us with gifts of pineapple and papaya.

Two hours later we left Keneyam and flew back into the mountains to inspect a newly-built clinic at Koroptak. The women came leaping into our arms, embracing us so exuberantly, delighted that we had come. They had so few visits and did not want us to leave."

As Elfrieda walked through the village, she stopped first at medical worker Martin's house. Several weeks previous his baby girl had been dying of dysentery. Martin remembered the Jeremiah 33:3 promise: Call to me, and I will answer you, and I will show you great and mighty things which you do not know. Obediently, he called on God to heal his little daughter. He was beaming as he told me the details of that miraculous event.

The next visit was at their houseboy's house. Their small baby, delivered by vacuum extraction at the government hospital in Wamena, now had a bump on her head. They were worried. Elfrieda put the baby over her shoulder, and the child promptly quieted for them to pray. She was able to reassure the parents that the swelling would dissipate with time.

Turnaround in Meneyem

Elfrieda documented the devastation of a false cult in the village of Meneyem medically.

> "When we visited Meneyem, most of the children were grossly malnourished at an emergency level. We put them on a high nutrition diet, supplementing it with lentils, oil, and salt to tempt their taste buds. Two tablespoons of oil a day provides certain weight gain."

Elfrieda returned three months later to discover that most of the children had not gained an ounce. The little one and two-year-old children had livers and spleens extending three to four fingers below their ribs, ballooning up their abdomens. Their faces were ashen, and their emaciated bodies racked with continuous fever.

What went wrong?

Questioning the parents revealed that a False Prophet Movement that began when a man named Pirion from the Juguru Valley became demon possessed had invaded Memeyem. It was spreading through other valleys like an epidemic. The people were both afraid of and attracted to the voices speaking to them through possessed villagers. It was comforting to hear a loved one's voice.

These evil spirits told the parents, "We are your medical helpers and pastors. Follow us." The parents were afraid to follow Elfrieda's instructions. Yet, they also did not want to become controlled by evil spirits. They were so desperate that all they wanted to do was drown themselves in the steep, rapidly-rushing rivers. The powers of darkness were at work in Meneyem.

"We told the parents that they should repent, confess and turn to the Lord. There was nothing else we could do. That evening after the service, seventy-five men, women and children stayed and began to confess and repent. Later, we joined in prayer together. Darianus, a medical worker, led in a time of renouncing the evil and reclaiming lost ground for the Lord.

In January, one month later, I needed to gather information to report to the government since they had helped fund the supplements we had given the people. Adi, another medical worker there, had faithfully administered the supplements for one month and then brought the reports to me, trekking over the trail to Mapnduma. He was beaming as he told me that an absolute miracle had occurred.

When I looked at the records, I discovered that twenty children showed major weight gain. I saw that two-year-old Ruana had gained nearly four kilos in one short month. Four-year-old Delfina outdid her, jumping from nine to fourteen point six kilos. Five-year-old Mandelena surpassed them all by gaining seven kilos in one month. I stared at the recorded weights in disbelief. Had the medical worker made a mistake? When the impact of what God had done hit me, my tears began to flow. Ours is a miracle-working God reaching out to all who will obey his Word, humble themselves and repent. He will lift them up."

From Near Death to Joyful Service

In desperation, Ani's mother rushed her nine-year-old daughter to Elfrieda's clinic wondering how much longer her precious child would be with her. Too sick to care, Ani lay on the hard clinic stretcher hovering between life and death. Her face had a deathly pallor. Her pulse was racing madly, and her head throbbed unmercifully.

With an overwhelming sense of urgency to save her life, Elfrieda examined her asking the Lord to give her wisdom to know what to do. For some time, Ani had been on iron injections, so Elfrieda checked her depleted IV shelf. She found a bottle of blood volume restorer. Now she needed to find a vein in Ani's thin arm. Because Ani was apprehensive about needles, they asked God to make the needle go into the vein easily.

When the needle went in, Ani didn't even wince. Smiling, she looked at Elfrieda as if to say, "That didn't even hurt!" What a precious little gem. Despite her weakness, she wanted to encourage the nurse. Ani survived that day, and all the necessary needle pokes she endured in the coming days.

Three weeks later, as the old oxygen tank was pounded to call the children to children's church, close to one hundred children came. Ani was with them, dressed in her newest grass skirt and colourful beads. It was an important day for her. She had received a personal invitation from Elfrieda to attend.

The children closely listened as Elfrieda explained the red page of the Wordless Book, telling the story about why Jesus came to die for them. In response to the invitation to accept the Lord Jesus as their Saviour, Ani was one of thirty-seven children who did so, praying, "O Lord, throw all the sin in my life behind your back. Come in and wash my heart clean with your precious blood. Thank you, Lord Jesus."

Years later, Ani became a nurse midwife. When she married Darianus, a nurse who trained under Elfrieda and then went on to government training to become a registered nurse, they committed themselves to become givers of life to the Nduga people caring for both physical and spiritual needs. They had no way of knowing at the time that Darianus would be the one to assume Elfrieda's leadership of the Nduga medical program.

Well-deserved Recognition

Elfrieda's work was gathering recognition beyond C&MA circles. In 1986, days before her wedding, Elfrieda was awarded the Robert W. Pierce Award for Christian Service, given each year to someone who serves the poor in a particular ministry in a single geographical area. She used the $10,000 grant to purchase medical supplies and cover helicopter fees for travel to the remote villages.

Adriaan, Elfrieda, Mrs. Lorraine Pierce

Elfrieda had become a legend for her energy, drive, and focused service. A life filled with the daily drama of broken bones and revolting scenes of stench, putrefaction, and death, Elfrieda did not flinch from pain or nauseating scenes. Hers is a story that stands alone.

Dr. Budi Hernawan, a lecturer at Paramadina Graduate School of Diplomacy Jakarta and widely recognized for his involvement in Papua peacebuilding, was aware of Elfrieda's vision and ability to implement changes necessary to improve the well-being of the Nduga people. It was Dr. Budi, interested in grassroots mission involvement, who facilitated putting Elfrieda's medical workers on government payroll, waiving the requirement that they attend government medical schools.

During one of the annual upgrading seminars required for the medical workers, Barbara Pillsbury, a medical/cultural anthropologist, flew in to observe Elfrieda's medical program. She was fascinated to see a culture so fresh out of the Stone Age, yet with trained medical workers so capable of caring for the sick.

Passing the Medical Mantle

In a 1991 Field Conference Report, Adriaan had commented on the result of Elfrieda's work.

> "The medical work is mostly delegated to our medical committee under Elfrieda's leadership. This committee makes all decisions, policies, placements, discipline, etc. She has trained more than eighty medical workers on several levels."

In 1995 it was time to hand over the administration of the medical training program at Mapnduma to the Ndugas.

> "On April 4, approximately 1,000 people gathered at the Mapnduma clinic. It was an honour to have Dr. Budi Hernawan present.
>
> My sermon topic was: The Good Shepherd Gives His Life for His Sheep. I urged every medical worker to be a good shepherd, giving both physical and spiritual care in their attending to the sick.

The medical workers came dressed in their former apparel of feather headdresses. The replacement of the headdress with modern-day ball caps acknowledged the change that had taken place from the Stone Age into the twentieth century. During the ceremony, Elfrieda was adorned with net bags, grass skirts, and beads and given an array of handouts including money gifts. It was an emotional day for her.

We have now passed on the medical mantle, under Darianus' leadership, to more than eighty faithful Nduga medical workers and midwives that we have trained over the past thirty-five years. Now the task is up to the Ndugas. New medical workers will receive medical training at government schools."

Lord, bless each one of these faithful medical workers with your lavish and plentiful rewards. You have called and equipped them to bring hope in despair, light to the darkness, healing to the sick, comfort to the dying. Give them wisdom. Give them the perseverance to remain faithful. May they finish well, giving you praise and glory. Amen.

12

THE BATTLE

THE UNSTOPPABLE CANADIAN NURSE was having her own bout of health issues. For the Ndugas, it was not easy to take. They had always seen this wiry, resilient woman as indomitable. Now they were discovering that she was human.

> "How quickly things change. We should be in the Mbuwa today ministering, but instead, we are making an unexpected trip to Kediri, Java for a biopsy. The Ndugas were quite upset and disappointed. Whatever the outcome, I want to become more like my Lord through this experience. I haven't had many personal blows besides Mijo's death, and probably the Lord thinks it is time for a few rough edges to be smoothed out. It turned out to be a minor incident compared to what was to come."

Dengue fever showed up.

> "It was September 1988 when I suddenly got sick. I laid flat for two solid weeks. The continuous high fevers caused total exhaustion, a

frequent choking sensation with no appetite, depression, dreadful backaches, and inability to concentrate. By October 10, it felt like my body was draining strength out of my bones, spine, and brain. I thought I would die. Adriaan was a great support and encouragement to me and prayed for the Lord's intervention."

Adriaan was well aware how hard it was for his wife to be still and rest.

"This dengue fever is something else. Many of our missionaries have had it. We have learned that recovery is slow, requiring much patience. Elfrieda struggles to take the time to rest and recover. Being in bed for almost three weeks was difficult for her. She kept having relapses. The fever did not go away. She lost a lot of weight, and her blood count was way down."

As Elfrieda rested, she began to receive letters that people had been praying for her in different areas of the world although they were oblivious of her need. Bonnie Douglas, a student at Canadian Bible College, said that for three months she had a special burden to pray for Elfrieda's health. She only heard later how sick Elfrieda had been. Lorraine Willems[2] wrote Elfrieda asking her what happened on October 10, 1988. Unaware of her desperate need Circle Drive Alliance Church in Saskatoon, Saskatchewan, set that day aside for fasting and prayer. God intervened.

"When people listen to the Lord, he reveals things to them. Life is so busy, and we forget that we are here to be a blessing and encouragement and not just to meet deadlines in getting the women's discipleship book done, or mimeographing the medical exam."

Then it was malaria. And the heat was sucking Elfrieda's energy away.

---

[2]Lorraine and her husband had been prayer warrior friends for decades and this reference indicates how involved they have been in prayer ministries and spiritual warfare for missionaries and pastors. Lorraine was the original spark to this book when she interviewed and recorded Adriaan and Elfrieda for what became the foundation of this book.

"Elfrieda is still tired and struggling with her health. As much as she wants to get going, she does not seem to be able to get as healthy as she wants. It has been very disheartening for her. We want to get to the bottom of this whole thing and may get some tests done somewhere where they know what they are doing."

It was Elfrieda's time to experience the solitude of a dark night of the soul.

"I have been so discouraged about my health, especially yesterday and then my Honey shared the verse God had given him in the morning from Matthew 11:30. Jesus said: My yoke is easy and my burden is light. It hit me like a bolt of lightning. I have been dragging the burden around with me all these weeks and burdening others with it. Jesus wants to carry it for me, so I decided to leave it with him, and he filled me with joy. We prayed together. God has blessed me by giving Adriaan to me. He is a consistent encouragement and so kind and loving a man to have around to share with."

The twenty-fifth anniversary of the entrance of the gospel into Ndugaland was fast approaching with big plans to celebrate. Three missionary couples planned on joining them for the celebration so Adriaan requested if Elfrieda's sister Elsie, who was teaching at the MK school in Sentani, could get a week off to come and help out at Mapnduma.

"Elsie was a godsend and like a ray of sunshine in our home. She busied herself with preparing the meals for the guests as well as helping take care of her sick sister. Then just before the celebration, she was called back to her teaching duties in Sentani. She was greatly missed."

The celebration was represented by all twelve major valleys of the Nduga population.

"On October 31, 1988, the Anniversary Celebration started. We had invited Rev. Obed Komba, our National Church leader, to be the guest speaker. He developed laryngitis and so, unexpectedly, that morning, I had to get a message together for the celebration. It must have been from the Lord because I felt anointed while speaking from Joshua 24:15. I quoted Joshua: Choose today whom you will serve. As for me and my family, we will serve the Lord. I spoke on the twelve stones, and since we have twelve valleys, a representative from each of the twelve valleys picked up a stone. Then they marched single file and piled up the stones under the Jesus banner before the Lord, as a pledge to keep serving him. It was a highlight and blessing as many consecrated their lives to follow God more closely."

The ability to improvise and never take himself too seriously sustained Adriaan over the years. Eventually, the combination of medical complications of both Adriaan and Elfrieda necessitated a medical leave for both. They turned their responsibilities over to others and left for a six-month furlough in February 1990. Their health was broken.

"During these past months, both of us have not been feeling well, which has been quite discouraging at times. Elfrieda has not been her old self since she came down with dengue fever. She still gets tired quickly, has to be careful in what she can do, which she finds very frustrating, having always been so very active."

Helping with physical needs had been Elfrieda's life, but the laboratory of the soul that Adriaan and Elfrieda were going through was orchestrated for a greater purpose. Their absences allowed their Nduga medical workers to incrementally realize that the mortality of the Dutch man, and his helpmate, was preparing them for the day when they would no longer be with them. It was this time in Canada that became the foundation for the deepest and most lasting ministry of the van der Bijls in their final years with the Ndugas.

When the van der Bijls returned to Canada, their mission doctor urged them to attend the C&MA Assembly in Quebec City, then stop in Toronto to have a consultation with their Tropical Disease specialist. At Assembly, among the hundreds of delegates, was an Alliance pastor, Rev. David Mitchell. He made himself available to them, and they talked together in their hotel room. Mitchell prayed with them and together they saw demonic curses broken and closed doorways that had innocently been opened to the deceitfulness of Satan. Elfrieda writes:

> "As we prayed, David Mitchell told me to search my heart and confess my sins and then, in the name of the Lord Jesus Christ, we broke the curses placed on me, and every spirit that was affecting me from within and without. We came against all the door openers to the enemy's bondage in my life—doorways innocently opened through traumatic experiences of fear, rejection, sin bondages, emotional areas, unforgiveness and spiritual blocks. We put the blood of Jesus between me and the evil one. David urged us to continue to surround ourselves with a wall of protection and cover ourselves with the blood of Jesus every day. When a curse was stated, I was to respond instantly, refusing, renouncing and cancelling the curse in the name of the Lord Jesus Christ and let God's power be demonstrated."

That time of spiritual warfare brought victory to her life.

> "I was set free! The heaviness weighing me down was gone. My heart was overflowing with joy, and I wanted to shout it from the housetops. I thank the Lord for every lesson learned during these months of sickness. It has equipped us with a wealth of spiritual understanding on how to fight the enemy that we want to share

with our Nduga people. I again realized the truth of Hosea 4:6 that my people are destroyed from lack of knowledge."

By August 1990, they were home in Mapnduma. Adriaan had been hopeful that they had passed a watershed but coming back into hostile enemy country reignited the battle. When the same fatigue and symptoms reappeared, Elfrieda wondered what she had done wrong.

> "Elfrieda has come back not as well as we would have liked. She is burned out and has to be careful about what she can do. When you see us going away from our station monthly and are wondering why, it is the doctor's order as a part of her therapy."

It did seem, however, that they had come into a new understanding of spiritual warfare.

> "The more we hear and read, the more we become aware of how ignorant we have been about our victory in Christ and the onslaught of the enemy in his territory these past twenty-seven years on the field. Many of us have not been serious about this and even shrugged it off out of fear or not wanting to be involved. However, whether we want to or not, we are involved."

Two years passed. In 1992, God in his mercy and perfect timing sent a team from Lighthouse Ministry International in Minneapolis, Minnesota to Papua to teach us about spiritual warfare. Their primary verse was James 4:7 which instructs: Submit yourselves therefore to God. Resist the devil, and he will flee from you. The emphasis was the authority we have in Christ and how we can take our stand against the evil one without fear and with boldness. Although Elfrieda had been delivered and healed while at home four years earlier, the closer she got to Papua, the more afflicted she felt. The Lighthouse Ministry team had an effective deliverance ministry. When they offered prayer, Adriaan and Elfrieda went for personalized ministry. Several things came to the surface. As they ministered, the team felt that a group of witches from Mapnduma were working against Elfrieda. In fact, a curse of death had been spoken over her.

The ministry of the Lighthouse Ministry team was similar to that of David Mitchell. They began with prayer and put on the armour of God according to Ephesians 6:10-18. Then they claimed the power of the blood of the Lord Jesus Christ and the authority of his name, invited the Holy Spirit to direct the ministry time, and claimed the victory in the name of the Lord Jesus Christ. Next, they went through door openers and permission to bind Satan. They broke all lineage strongholds back to the third and fourth generation in the name of the Lord Jesus Christ. They severed all communication between Satan and evil spirits in the name of the Lord Jesus Christ and broke the curses. As each sin was confessed, the enemy's hold was resisted and rebuked, and the Holy Spirit invited to occupy all areas of freedom.

"After that session, I felt so free and clean inside. I wanted nothing to contaminate me again. I felt a new freedom in my life as never before. The team urged us to resist the evil forces every time the symptoms returned. It happened many times, but I now knew how to resist Satan in the authority and name of the Lord Jesus Christ.

When we returned to Mapnduma the following week, we told the Nduga church leaders about the deliverance we experienced. They were excited and reminded us that they had asked us to teach and assist them with spiritual warfare since we first arrived at Mapnduma many years ago."

Alone and Vulnerable

It was only in the throes of Adriaan's final year in Mapnduma that Satan unleashed the full force of his unbridled fury on him. The battle began first with Elfrieda. He felt the sting most directly in an attack on his wife.

On a night when Elfrieda found herself alone in Mapnduma, she began to feel vulnerable. They had not wanted it to happen. Now, even the elements conspired against them, and they were separated by weather.

"Tonight I am in Mapnduma, alone, in a place where I would not choose to be. But God allowed it to keep me trusting him continually for victory. The plan was to stop in the Mbuwa and pick up Adriaan. However, the Mbuwa was closed in with weather. So we went on to Mapnduma. There is so much heaviness here at Mapnduma."

It was not to be, and Elfrieda felt fear and isolation. Adriaan was not there when she needed him. Instead, the place that had been her place of security and comfort and home for twenty-seven years became a place of concern. She withstood the night, but it was a lesson on how the enemy works to send terror in the night and how the Lord gives wisdom to stand strong when the storms come.

Elfrieda did not grow quickly into the dynamics at play in her life, and for her life. Her journey into the reality of spiritual warfare began through a comment by a professor in Canadian Bible College days. When Elfrieda was ready to leave for the mission field, Professor Ray Kincheloe communicated to her a very helpful truth that became a lifeline that she clung to when she realized she was over her depth in a dark land, still very much ruled by Satan. According to Revelation 12:11, they overcame him by the blood of the Lamb. He suggested that she make this verse a powerful prayer to always cover herself with the blood of the Lord Jesus Christ as her protection from the attack of the enemy.

She remembered his comments when, as an always upbeat confident worker, she was suddenly struck by hopeless depression that refused to lift. She remembered the words when women in the tribe broached her with the rumour that she had been cursed by witches who vowed that she would die. She remembered the words that night alone in the dark Mapnduma night when she saw great balls of fire cascading out of the darkness circling and surrounding the boundary fence of her home.

> "I committed my night into the Lord's hands. As usual, I prayed a prayer of protection to envelope me in his presence and surround me:
>
> Father, in the mighty name of the Lord Jesus Christ, I ask that the blood of the Lord Jesus Christ of Nazareth cover my body, home, and family tonight. In your mighty name, Father, I ask you to assign your warrior angels with swords of light to surround me, our home inside and outside the boundaries of our property and protect, defend, and preserve me from the enemy. I thank you, Father, that you are a very present help. You never leave us or forsake us, and you are my deliverer! I thank you for victory, complete and total in this situation, for your glory, honour, and praise. Amen.

Later that night, I went to the bathroom. As I looked out of the window, I saw what looked like balls of fire flying outside the stone fence that surrounded that part of our home. I stared in disbelief and then realized they were outside the boundary of our property as I had prayed. I went back to bed thanking and praising the Lord for his protection and went right to sleep.

Psalm 91:4 tells me that God will cover me with his feathers. He will shelter me with his wings. His faithful promises are my armour and protection. I am still in awe of such reassurance. But we have to ask."

Mending the Fences

Elfrieda was not the only one in Ndugaland learning about spiritual warfare.

"Lewi, my medical worker sent an emergency medical radio message that his wife, Dorti, my top-notch midwife, had been unconscious for eleven days. He was in tears. He indicated that it was witchcraft, so we prayed.

After Lewi called me, he searched his heart. He had about ten pigs and piglets, and they were always mulling around the yard and airstrip, and not behind the fence as they should be. He had known that was not correct, telling me that he had not kept his heart clean and now the Lord has not heard his prayers. The pigs were a danger to incoming aircraft. Convicted, he killed them all."

That lesson encouraged Elfrieda that some people were listening to God and little things are big things to a sensitive heart. It was not a matter of keeping the pigs penned up. It was about disobedience. It was a lesson learned. He killed the pigs. Whatever gets between God and us is sin. Because he stepped out in obedience, God answered Lewi's prayer and his wife recovered.

Elfrieda took the lesson for herself.

"The fences of our lives need to be mended. Our feeble defences need to be shored up against the forces of evil because wherever the enemy gets a foothold, he will enter and destroy."

In her head, Elfrieda knew Satan does not want to give up his strongholds. But she had also learned to daily trust the Holy Spirit to lead her
into all truth and to walk under his guidance to see great and mighty things
accomplished. Zechariah 4:6 says: Not by might, nor by power, but by my
Spirit, says the Lord Almighty.

The Intercessors

What sustained Adriaan and Elfrieda through the years was an army of inter-
cessors. Among them was her sister Anna. Elfrieda described her as the prayer
warrior. Anna had linked with a Nduga pastor when his mother died. The pastor, Josias, was distraught that his precious praying mother was now gone.
Who would support him through his ministry which was at times so difficult?
When Anna read of his plight in one of Elfrieda's letters she sent word to as-
sure him that she would take over the prayer ministry where his dear mother
had left off. Neither distance nor culture nor language impeded the flow of
spiritual energy that radiated throughout the valley through Anna's prayers.

"When I was preparing to leave for Irian, my sister Anna gave me
a tract, Victory Now through Prayer and Persevering Praise. She
gave testimony as to how praise had revolutionized her life. Anna
reminded me of two verses. 1 Thessalonians 5:18 was one: Give
thanks in all circumstances, for this is God's will for you in Christ
Jesus. Psalm 34:1 was the other one: Extol the Lord at all times;
his praise will always be on my lips.

When tribal war broke out in the Mugi Valley, a full day's
walk from Mapnduma, a group of pastors decided to intercept the
feud. We called them into our home for prayer and shared from 2
Chronicles 20:17, 22 how God guided Jehoshaphat to victory: You
will not have to fight this battle. Take up your positions. Stand firm
and see the deliverance the Lord will give you. As they began to
sing and praise, the Lord set ambushes against the men and they
were defeated. The destruction was so complete that Jehoshaphat
and his army never met the enemy.

In the wake of this new revolt in the Mugi, we sought God
and committed the dispute into his hands with thanksgiving and
praise to him for the victory. The men left, and we continued to

pray before the Lord. When the pastors arrived in Mugi, the problem had dissolved. God had intervened amazingly through the weapon of persevering praise."

Anna Toews Krahenbil with Pastor Josias

Spiritual warfare can never be matter-of-fact, but Adriaan and Elfrieda had learned to fight back with all the spiritual weapons the Lord had given them. Sometimes it became almost as natural as breathing and just as necessary. Always their focus was on Jesus and the victory he provides.

Witch Hunt

The intertwining of medical science with supernatural manifestations is for some a bizarre and incompatible mix but in Papua, the two often collided. Elfrieda was a consummate professional who did all she could to help people who needed her medical expertise. Still, there were times when she realized she was dealing with something much larger than clinical capability.

For North American sensibilities this stuff is more like a Hollywood horror script than a documentary. For many people in the civilized West, who espouse a worldview that borders on the trite, this is rather heady stuff, if not medieval. From a Christian perspective, spiritual warfare is the cosmic war of good versus evil. For Elfrieda and Adriaan, they fought its battles daily. It was a reality they did not learn about early on. It almost cost them their lives.

The drama of life and death plays itself out on the slopes of Ndugaland daily. What was a commonplace occurrence for the van der Bijls was a strange and scary phenomenon for visitors who ventured unknowingly into Ndugaland. A Canadian executive learned the hard way. He fancied himself an adventurer who was up for anything, but this was more than he anticipated. Witches were a way of life in the highlands, and when he landed in Mapnduma, he was not in some idyllic hinterland but a spiritual war zone.

Witch hunts were common in the Nduga lifestyle. A woman could exercise power or control over a man by calling on evil powers to help her. So, men were often on the lookout for suspected witches. Sometimes they relied on the unexpected to announce who the witches were. Or they might use supernatural signs or tribal lore to identify the sorceress. At the fire pit, if the sweet potatoes cooked less on one side than the other, it could point in the direction of a witch.

All this became too much for the newly-arrived visitor. He was left alone as Adriaan attended to an incident where a young man had suddenly gone crazy, grabbed his weapons and was now on the loose. Elfrieda invited him into a small kitchen where women, in their grass skirts, were preparing for a pig feast. He took one look into the kitchen and refused to enter.

That afternoon word came that six women were being held hostage as witches in a village across the river. The visitor, already uneasy from the morning's events, locked his bedroom door and refused to come out, even when the ruckus subsided, and it was time for him to meet the pastors who had gathered expectantly in the van der Bijl's living room. He was relieved when the plane landed the following morning to fly him out.

A Strange Mix

Sometimes the interplay of spiritual battles and truculent sinners made for a strange mix. Elfrieda described this mix during a prayer ministry seminar.

"The Ndugas face various temptations including not reading the

Word, the desire to take another wife, not praying faithfully, discouragement when someone dies, killing a wife, falling asleep when praying or reading the Word, anger, not doing what the pastor says."

Putting the desire for another wife in the same breath as falling asleep while praying might seem a little radical, but Elfrieda equated the temptations of discouragement when someone dies right alongside killing a wife. It sounds like the Sermon on the Mount. All these things, big and small, were obstacles to maturity that these men and women battled daily. There was no need to differentiate the size of the sin.

These little incidental misdemeanours could hardly be lumped in with the bigger sin of wife killing, could they? Adriaan and Elfrieda spoke of them in the same breath. It was life in the raw where black and white was preferred to shades of grey when it came to disobedience.

"A pastor's daughter had an affair with a young man, so they were expelled from school. There was a big hoopla about the expulsion to the point that she threatened to throw herself in the river if she couldn't go back to school.

Our houseboy joined a crowd with his bow and arrows to settle a dispute and was disciplined for allowing this carnality to surface."

The connection between bad behaviour and deep spiritual currents in a culture that prevented men and women from making a clean break with the past was dawning on Elfrieda and Adriaan. They were beginning to grasp that an undercurrent of evil kept Mapnduma in the clutches of evil powers.

"Mapnduma seems to be known for sudden deaths. Several church leaders are thinking of taking second wives. Evil is on the rampage."

It was time to take proactive steps although they were unsure of the ground they were treading. When the first forays into the spiritual dimensions of this underworld became apparent, they began to fast on Sundays.

"Many of Satan's victims do not know there is a war going on. They make easy prey. People need to know that we are in the middle of a great spiritual struggle. Even more distressing is that many do not understand the nature of Satan's schemes, the weapons he employs, and more importantly the weapons which God has provided for our protection. I preached on Ephesians 6:10-20 which is the clearest definition of spiritual warfare in Paul's writings. It not only tells us that there is a spiritual war, but it warns us that apart from utilizing the weapons which God has provided we are hopelessly underpowered.

Twenty people came forward asking prayer for discernment. Several leaders joined me to pray and asked me to counsel them."

Elfrieda recognized how deeply the women were affected.

"During the weekend ladies' retreat, I spoke on spiritual warfare and prayer. We had ninety-five women from fifteen churches. We encouraged them to memorize ten verses of Scripture during the retreat. Three women did it. One of the women learned the verses even though she had to trek back and forth to her village every night during the entire retreat."

Like the church worldwide, many were still so bound up in their carnal lifestyle that it took a mighty work of the Holy Spirit to tear down the walls and bring a spiritual breakthrough. The van der Bijls were so grateful for faithful pastors, school teachers, and medical workers who stood up for the truth. They lived and taught that example in more than ninety village churches throughout Ndugaland in the power of the Holy Spirit who works as we allow him to do so.

Marriage Complications

Women's work was not designed to be an afterthought, but a cultural clue into unlocking the chains that bound the Nduga tribe.

"I had a good time with about fifty to sixty women training them how to become godly Christian women and anointed leaders in their ministry to other women. On the last day, we called the pastors to encircle the women, give them their support, and pray for them. The men had been opposing the women's work. One lady spoke for the women pointing out that formerly it was their job to raise the children and tend to the pigs. But now that the gospel has come, they want to reach out. They were asking the men to babysit while they spend time mentoring the village women.

The men stood up and gave the women their full support. They invited the ladies to join the rice feast. It was a significant advance when women, who had been good only for child raising and pig tending, were given special honour at this feast. Many of the women, full of zeal for the Lord, were so charged they also prayed for the sick, reporting the miracles God was doing."

The women would no longer take no for an answer.

"With the husbands involved in the pastoral upgrading school, the wives came and wanted to be taught as well. Two wives came to the men's classes and did not take no for an answer. As a result, we began a course for them that day. We chose an excellent discipleship course, Following Jesus. It boosted their faith and confidence as they joined their husband-pastors to minister in their village churches."

The struggle was not always of epic proportions. The little issues that afflict the church in any place were also present.

"The vice-chair of the Mapnduma ladies' ministry continued to be unrepentant for the hurts she had caused and is threatening to marry another man if she is not reelected to her position on the women's committee. There was so much tension, disputing, and backbiting in the old committee that it was clear we needed new leadership. Everybody was afraid it would upset the old leadership, but it went smoothly when a new group of women was elected."

The temptation to take other wives or marry another man was a latent threat that sometimes surfaced when things did not go the way people planned. Orit Kwe, a mature women's leader, discerned a spirit of carnality and bitter rivalry behind the threat that blocked blessing in the church. She spoke out against this spirit in a sweet, eloquent way. She got up after the sermon, took a sweet potato vine and said that only the immediate vine bears a blossom. That is like a husband and wife. The rest of the vines that sprout off do not bear. They are like other wives. It made an impact.

The need to reinforce Christian marriage was constant. Fidelity was valued in the Nduga culture. They frowned on promiscuity. Adultery usually triggered a war. Men took other wives, but it was not the norm. If sexual intimacy was at a premium in a Stone Age culture, sexual license was not. Marriage was carefully shrouded in privacy.

One of the reasons that Mijo, Mary, and Elfrieda found women's ministry so slow at the start is that the men were afraid that even in the church witches might be present. Despite the low view of women when Adriaan, Mijo, Mary, and Elfrieda arrived, breaking through to the women became an important step to the redemption of the culture. The marriage seminar was a successful step in teaching them that spiritual growth is the job of both husband and wife. They needed to be spiritually connected to work together to build a godly family.

Dreams and Visions

Anas, at one time Elfrieda and Mary's houseboy, now a pastor, talked about a dream he had before he was assigned to his first church in Yingginat, west of Mapnduma. Someone in the dream called, "Anas, come quickly. I have something to tell you. Get your family." Anas gathered the family together. They bowed their heads. Then, from a large bottle, the person poured red fluid onto the family. When he closed the bottle, he said, "Now go to the place assigned to you." The next morning, Anas was assigned to the church at Yingginat.

While Anas was at that church, a twelve-year-old boy, Som, got very sick and became unconscious. As Som lay dying, Anas and his wife, Sara, prayed. The boy began to shake and opened his eyes and told them he was thirsty. He revived after he ate the sugar cane they gave him.

Anas told him about John 3:16 and God's love and how God makes life worth living. The youngster decided to follow the One who gave his life to save him.

Just before Anas returned to Mapnduma, his little three-year-old girl, Jarni, had fallen victim to cerebral malaria. She was deathly ill, and her body had turned cold. People warned him to pay his debts, but he replied that he had no debts. Anas thought, "God anointed me for the ministry and he will provide. He can give me my Jarni back, or he can take her. That is his decision." They had Atenus, the medical worker, join them for a time of intercession. As they prayed, Anas noticed the veins distend with blood in Jarni's little feet as her circulation returned. She opened her eyes and asked for water. Rejoicing, Anas praised the Lord for the miracle of his daughter's restored life.

Martin, a medical worker and children's leader, told of the times when God provided for him. While in high school, he was starving. He called on God who provided through a lady who came up to him, dropped her net with the sweet potatoes she was taking to the market and went on her way.

Later in life, when nursing in a village, Martin lost consciousness and was dying. People gathered to pray for him. Suddenly, while they were praying, a brilliant multi-coloured beam of light from the heavens shone right onto the place where he lay in the hut. He felt life coming into his feet and inching its way up his body. He stirred, sat up, and jumped to his feet. "I'm healed. God healed me!" he shouted.

For a reserved Dutch guy like Adriaan, there was a side that did not always show through in his demeanour. Elfrieda had Mennonite roots; Adriaan came from a Dutch Reformed persuasion. There was little to suggest that they would probably be more comfortable in a charismatic community than a high church congregation. So where did this bent come from? Both Adriaan and Elfrieda say that they were most likely influenced in that direction by the Nduga people, a people of dreams and visions. They imbibed the atmosphere of the spiritual reality that surrounded them.

Now it was time to wade deeper into the water.

> "Adriaan is in bed with what we hope is not Dengue Fever. He got a headache on Valentine's Day at Pogapa, John and Joy Cutt's station. We did blood smears and gave him malaria medicine, but his temperature is elevated, he has persistent headaches and back discomfort, perspires a lot with decreased appetite and is very tired."

This illness had been foreshadowed to Adriaan in a dream a day before. He was learning to listen to this prompting.

> "In a vision the Lord showed me, I saw Jesus riding on a white horse coming down the path. Scary creatures were lurking around our home, and when they saw King Jesus, they retreated. Then the horse jumped into our yard. The glory of the Lord covered our house and then lifted and spread over the entire Nduga tribe."

These insights into the spiritual reality around them gave Adriaan and Elfrieda confidence and hope.

> "The vision was precious and brought Jesus so close to us. We realized the importance of spending much time in prayer and praise because it is through worship and praise that the enemy's power is disturbed."

Sometimes the dreams communicated truth. At other times they consoled or encouraged. Adriaan and Elfrieda often considered themselves in kindergarten when it came to war zone warfare and confronting evil giants in the valley. These dreams and visions became a gentle foreshadow that they would use as they battled on the enemy's turf, but not on the enemy's terms.

13

LIFE ON THE RUN

THE HUMDRUM OF ROUTINE was rarely an issue in Mapnduma. Regular interruptions crowded into the van der Bijl days to demand attention and God-given wisdom. It was more usual that interruptions were spiced with occasional commonplace than the other way around.

Today the drone of the generator and the click-clack of the mimeograph was all that separated Adriaan from boredom. His life was a maze of nonstop decisions and situations clamoring for immediate attention interspersed with the ordinary. He waited days for the weather to clear so he could fly. There was always something to do, and today he was filling his hours with helping copy a book on spiritual warfare. When the clouds lifted, he would try to recuperate the loss of time and the demands that had now hit fever pitch.

This chapter gives us a look at the van der Bijl calendar and some insight into their life and work in Papua. It is a matter of fact. It is understated. It is direct. The details indicate a holistic focus to their approach. They were well ahead of the trend toward compassion and justice in the C&MA international ministries.

A Typical Year's Dizzying Calendar

Adriaan and Elfrieda were in some ways wired for each other. Each had an appetite for work, a high energy level—when dengue or malaria had not slowed them down—and an incessant drive to accomplish the Lord's work. Their strength was also their weakness. For them, rest was not always a high value.

A typical year's activity looks like a laundry list for a physical breakdown.

January 30-February 11 - Elfrieda hosted the senior medical staff seminar in the Mbuwa. The theme: Seek First the Kingdom of God.

March 3-13 - Adriaan facilitated a Sion Bible School seminar at Pyramid.

March 23-30 - Adriaan responsible for a grade school teacher's seminar.

April 1-8 – Elfrieda directed a medical seminar in the Keneyam. Adriaan travelled to visit the Bible Schools in Indonesia as Education Co-ordinator.

These were large chunks of time that involved preparation, energetic involvement in complex interpersonal relationships, and major funding and personnel decisions.

April 16 – Ladies retreat. A new ladies' committee was elected without incident.

May 6-8 – Elfrieda attends a translation workshop in Sentani to learn how to translate a book on family planning into the Nduga language. Adriaan addressed boy-girl issues in the Nduga dorm in Abepura.

May 11-14 – Adriaan ministered to pastors in Silimo. Elfrieda connected with the ladies.

May 15 – Home in Mapnduma. Elfrieda facilitates a mini upgrading medical workers seminar.

May 28-September 4 – A short furlough to the United States and Canada required to renew Adriaan's green card. Visiting family in Washington State and Tennessee. Spending time in Saskatoon, Saskatchewan. Speaking in several churches.

September 6-11 - Adriaan is involved in the Executive Committee

meeting in Jayapura which takes care of C&MA mission mat-
ters in-between annual field conferences.

September 15 – Repairing damage done during a lightning storm.
Radio aerial struck by lightning. Two 55-gallon water drums
at the clinic fell off the stands.

September 17-22 - Church conference in Enarotali in the Wissel
Lakes area, including the election of a new church president
for Papua.

September 24-30 – Nursing Seminar at Pyramid for all Indonesian
and expat doctors and nurses in the developing world to upgrade and integrate important medical advances.

October 1 – Elfrieda met with medical staff to discuss next year's
goals.

October 2 – Mini-Seminar with the Sunday School teachers.
Topic: How to Teach.

October 6-10 – An Nduga medical seminar at Mapnduma for
medical workers, midwives, mother/child care workers. The
eighty medical workers gathered for upgrading, graduation,
and assignments to new outposts. The theme: Being a Good
Samaritan. Spiritually enriched and with new supplies of medicines, they returned to their village clinics to serve needy people.

October 16 – Immigration called Adriaan to Jayapura for finger printing.

October 19 - Upgrading Bible School discipleship courses for Nduga pastors.

October 23 – Ladies Retreat in Mbuwa. Adriaan speaks on Spiritual Warfare. Elfrieda gives medical advice to ninety-five women from fifteen churches.

November 2 - New nursing course at Mapnduma for upgrading the twelve medical workers who have been working in the field for three years.

November 5 – Elfrieda teaches sixty children in Children's Church. Twenty-nine decisions for Christ.

November 6 – Adriaan goes to Alama Valley via helicopter with an evangelistic team to visit churches in the area. He examines the airstrip.

November 16 – A new medical workers class begins.

November 17 – Adriaan and Elfrieda visit outposts by helicopter and oversee village churches.

November 19 – Pig feast for Adriaan's birthday.
    December 25 – Celebrated Christmas at Sentani.
    December 26 – Home to Mapnduma.

A Typical Two-Week Trip

There is no way to describe what a typical trip for Adriaan might be like, but a Tigi visit in the Wissel Lakes area highlights the broad range of activities and situations that he regularly facilitated. This trip was a journey down memory lane for Adriaan. It was where he had served during his three years as Superintendent of the Indonesian schools for grades one to six before assignment to the Nduga tribe in Mapnduma.

> "We decided that I should go with Adriaan to Tigi to settle some personnel issues between the school teachers. Tigi is an Ekari tribal station where Adriaan and Mijo first landed when he was Superintendent of Schools in 1960."

The trip took two weeks. They left Mapnduma, landed at various stations, and finally arrived at the Wagaite airstrip.

"A black cloud had formed over the lake followed by a heavy downpour. The Tigi people knew we would have to wait until the rain subsided before we could take the boat across the lake.

At four p.m. the rain stopped. We packed up and walked down the airstrip to the motorboat. It was tied up in a muddy inlet. Adriaan helped paddle us to the river, and finally, after more than ten tries, we got the motor going. After an hour on the lake, we arrived at Tigi.

The entire village came out to welcome us. Adriaan's last visit was a year ago. No missionary had visited them since. I couldn't contain my tears when I saw them ecstatically welcoming us. The crowd was overjoyed as they escorted us to the house where we would stay. They had prepared a fully-furnished, freshly-cleaned home for us.

In the morning we woke up to the sound of angry voices in front of the house. We hurried downstairs and saw the entire village assembled at the front door. The people had gathered to voice their frustration and concerns with rising prices. I guess they had no one to complain to, so they confronted us. We faced a group of men, women, and children, along with their goats, shouting and screaming their complaints. Later that day, Adriaan had to deal with a jealousy problem between two school teachers. It took prayer and godly wisdom to resolve the dispute."

The next morning, Adriaan and Elfrieda again crossed the lake to catch their plane at the Wagaite airstrip. They waited all day. The plane never arrived.

For Adriaan and Elfrieda, making the most of delays and detours was part of a typical day. They made the best of the situation. Elfrieda put her typical positive spin on a disappointing turn to the trip, by transforming the dilapidated house near the airstrip in Wagaite into a personal love nest for the night.

"We cleaned out the rat-infested trailhouse, added a few cushions to the single mattress that was there and found that it became a comfortable bed. We had a lovely, quiet evening together."

The plane arrived the next day. Adriaan and Elfrieda travelled to Nabire where Adriaan attended a board meeting.

The following day they were off to Pogapa where Elfrieda's nesting kicked in when they visited John and Joy Cutts' station. It was a dream home, with a fireplace and bay windows. Elfrieda thought it was fixed up so cute and dreamed about having a retreat home like it someday. John had three ultra-light planes that allowed him to move around freely, hopping from village to village over the mountains enabling him to avoid long treks.

Back home after the trip to Tigi, there was no rest in sight.

Sidebar

This little sidebar about their work, added as an aside indicates their workload and ministry approach. The line begins with a sly one-word addition—also.

"Also, using the helicopter, we plan to visit some of our thirty Nduga clinics and have evangelistic meetings in the village churches. We will show the Jesus Film. To people who have never seen a film, it was like Jesus had come to their village. It brought tears to their eyes and refreshing to their spiritual lives."

Visiting thirty far-flung clinics, even by helicopter, was a daunting task. These were not courtesy calls. Invariably, it involved dealing with serious issues the medical workers were facing. They needed advice or resolution. Adriaan was good at problem-solving and funding conundrums.

> "What used to take days and weeks of trekking is now accomplished in hours by helicopter. Visiting churches, discipling and ministering has become much more efficient and fruitful. More time can now be spent fellowshipping with the Ndugas in their villages."

Change of Pace

> "We went to the coast for a Translation Workshop that Elfrieda attended to translate a book on family life into the Nduga language. I went with her and was on the road most of the time during the week."

At the coast, Elsie needed a vehicle, so Adriaan shopped for one in Jayapura. He soon drove up with a Toyota van in good condition. Elsie was involved in youth ministries, and the van was exactly what she needed. But it called for a carport. Adriaan promptly ordered lumber and needed supplies. Before he went back to the interior, he arranged for several carpenters to build the carport. Elsie was surprised at how smoothly it all happened.

Sometimes Adriaan and Elfrieda were able to collaborate their schedules, but often they were moving in opposite directions. Yet, they were never happier than when they were active and involved in discipleship ministry. The secret to their marriage and ministry was the ability to find de-stressors along the way and, of course, to have Bible study and prayer together each day.

"We are now in Silimo overseeing the Maxey station while they are on furlough. We do not know how much we can do effectively covering such a large area. With the Lord's guidance, we will do what we can. I will minister to the pastors and Elfrieda will connect with the ladies.

Elfrieda is working on an Operation Impact course offered to missionaries by Azusa Pacific University in the United States. She was able to complete her master's degree in Papua with four professors from the United States coming every year to facilitate a week of concentrated teaching. The principles are incorporated into the Ndugas' ministries in creative ways during the year. We are happy to be here. It is a cozy place with a big fireplace. There is a little hydro, so we have twenty-four/seven electricity. We have had precious fellowship with the Silimo people while here. It is rewarding."

The Schools

A major educational component of Adriaan's portfolio was managing the government schools. He had been doing this since teaching at Wissel Lakes, and before that observed his father's expertise in this area. He understood the Indonesian school system like the back of his hand. He moved from school to school, and problem to problem, with an ease that belied the complexity of each situation.

"Our government schools keep on running understaffed and every year brings more hassle. This results in more students flocking to the interior city of Wamena, and on to the coast at Sentani and Abepura. As we see many of them flounder and get sucked up into the mainstream of the world, it compels us to help. Dorms are not the only answer, but they serve to guide and encourage the students spiritually as they get their education."

Adriaan, as Community Development Coordinator for the region, had been looking into funding a dorm in Wamena for students from the tribes in the mountain areas. He had managed to broker purchasing land in Wamena, and his dream was to create an educational institution for the mountain dwellers in their area. He believed strongly in investing in the youth of the region to fuel the leaders of tomorrow.

The educational aspect of running scattered schools and medical programs and clinics was a God-given challenge. Added to the responsibility was the duty to spearhead community development. When you are an army of one, everything falls on your plate.

"We now have three Nduga government clinics, fifteen mission clinics and fifteen village health centers mostly built with funds from Holland. World Relief Canada is currently helping with the funding of medical supplies for these clinics as well as cables for upgrading swinging bridges.

Through our community development program, we have a hydro project completed in the Mbuwa Valley. This services our home with twenty-four/seven electricity, as well as the clinic, youth center, church, teachers and medical workers homes. The Mbuwa is the most heavily populated valley among the Ndugas, so we need to spend longer periods of time among these people who are open and eager for ministry. It has warranted building a house, which has turned into a cozy honeymoon cottage at an altitude of 6,500 feet in the Mbuwa."

The irony was that there was a cozy honeymoon cottage at a comfortable altitude but little time to enjoy it unless company came. They were never happier than when stretched to the limit of their endurance.

"Our days are full and satisfying. God is on our side and giving us daily strength and guidance. With at least 1,000 people milling around, and teaching programs going on, it is exciting to see the people content and enjoying themselves."

Purse Strings

The elephant in the room of cross-cultural mission work has always been the finances. Who do you give to, when do you give, and how much? When is enough too much and when is all you have still not enough? The battle to fund the right projects and give to the right people was a drain on Adriaan though he seemed to weather the stressors well.

Although it was always difficult to distinguish true need from the unnecessary handout, Adriaan seemed to err on the side of generosity.

Even pig feasts that seemed like an inordinate waste to Adriaan for people teetering on the brink of starvation were necessary expenditures. He understood their cultural significance to the Ndugas and often funded or supported lavish feasts where the number of pigs killed measured the success of the feast. On one occasion he reported,

> "I arranged for tons of rice to be available because of the current potato shortage. An oil company working here provided more than 1,000 pounds of rice as a gift and sold us more at a very reasonable price."

To Adriaan, hardened by the knocks and deceptions of thirty-three years of rubbing shoulders with the freeloaders among the Ndugas, the next handout was almost a reflex response. He seemed to be able to screen the requests and sort through the needs with ease. Being the dispenser of goods and services was not a mantle that Adriaan relished. From the beginning, the role had been thrust on him by circumstance. He wore the mantle begrudgingly, but with grace.

14

PAPUA'S LIFELINE

THERE WAS A TRUST IN THE LORD in the way Adriaan approached the danger and uncertainty of flying in hazardous and inhospitable conditions. What had taken him two weeks to trek through the valleys, crossing rushing rivers and climbing over the rugged mountains on his first trip to Mapnduma could now be accomplished in minutes.

A pilot could fly over the mountains to drop off several cases of Nduga Bibles for one village and land to drop off a passenger at another village if weather conditions were favourable. MAF was a lifeline for ministry in Papua.

> "The friendly MAF pilot was our newspaper of sorts, relaying what was happening in the outside world. When MAF pilot George Boggs dropped in with the much-looked-for mail and then stayed to join us for tea, he was a ray of sunshine and encouragement to us. At the airstrip, he prayed with us before taking off.
>
> Dorti, Elfrieda's midwife, commented that the pilot must be a Christian. He had set a good example in speech and conduct to inspire the onlookers."

The missionaries were always on radio standby when a pilot made the first landing at a freshly opened airstrip.

> "Bob Johanson reported landing on the newly completed airstrip at Wandama in the lowlands south of Mapnduma. Then there was silence. Very concerned, we stood by the radio with bated breath,

hoping he had landed safely. We waited for what seemed an hour. We learned that after Bob landed, he made a friendly visit to each hut to fellowship with the jubilant Ndugas there. He called it his David Livingston Experience. He will surely be rewarded with a Well done, good and faithful servant."

The downside was the constant dependence on weather. Adriaan learned to adjust his itinerary to what the skies allowed, but he was not always pleased with the waiting. The weather window into Mapnduma was extremely narrow. Flights did not come in after nine a.m. when fog frequently shrouded the valley and unpredictable wind gusts made landing treacherous. MAF could not airlift medical emergencies out after nine in the morning. This restriction is why the advent of helicopter service, with its ability to beat the weather into submission and land in tight spots, was a major upgrade.

Close Calls

Life in the highlands was dangerous. Risk was everywhere, and tragedy as near as the next take-off.

Mary and Elfrieda along with Martin, one of Elfrieda's medical workers, boarded the one-engine Cessna at Mapnduma. They were on their way to celebrate Christmas at Sentani. After the plane took off a storm closed in around them. The pilot was unfamiliar with the area. The pass over the high ranges was closed, so he began to fly from east to west and back again.

> "We were sitting behind him. He turned around to tell us that if we saw anything familiar, we should let him know. There was nothing to see. We were both cold with fright. We watched the gas tanks switch from an empty one to a full one. Then that second tank dipped close to empty.
>
> I knew I was ready to meet my Lord, but I wondered how it would happen. I recommitted my life into his hands. The Lord brought Isaiah 41:10 to mind: Fear not I am with you; do not be dismayed, for I am your God. I will strengthen you and help you; I will uphold you with my righteous right hand. My heart filled with peace and I began to praise the Lord silently for his enabling. We knew the pilot was talking to other pilots on his radio, but

we could not hear the conversation. I looked out the window, and there in the distance, I saw it. I grabbed Mary's arm. Look! There's a plane.

MAF pilot John Miller was God's angel of rescue. He led our plane to a MAF base. As we landed, the second fuel tank recorded empty! God still has work for us to do."

• It was on a Saturday morning. Elfrieda, along with guests Jerry and Jeannie Lynn, boarded a MAF 206 Cessna with MAF pilot Mike Brooks. Adriaan was to come on the next flight. They enjoyed the flight over the towering jagged mountains, through the pass, and then over to the Mbuwa. After landing, unloading and reloading a pig into the pod—MAF had designed a pod which was moulded around and attached to the underbelly of the plane for smaller items and small livestock—Mike was on his way to his next landing.

"I took the Lynns to the house, not knowing if I would see Adriaan that day or not. The Lynns were enjoying our lovely Mbuwa honeymoon cottage when minutes later the plane was back on the runway. We ran out, and there was Mike, revving his engine. He told us that, as he was ascending, trying to gain altitude to go through the pass and on to Pyramid for Adriaan, the turbo engine lost power. He had just enough time to maneuver the plane back onto the Mbuwa runway.

He removed the hood and saw that a tube had blown off. We invited Mike in for a refreshing drink and a time to relax. He broke down with the emotion of the near miss. It was a close call."

Mike called MAF pilot Tom Bolser to come with tools to fix the crippled plane. Tom flew by Pyramid to pick up Adriaan on his way. The plane got fixed, and they left. Five days later Mike was landing at another airstrip when his brakes failed, and the plane almost overshot the airstrip with a 3,000-foot drop-off at the end. For the second time, pilot Mike praised God for his almighty power at work in protecting him from certain danger.

• Jerry Reeder crashed in the Ilaga Valley. He was rolling down the strip, but when he tried to take off, he had no power. He crashed into a sweet potato field and barely had time to crawl out before the plane burst into flames. The plane was a total loss. Fortunately, there were no passengers on board.

• MAF pilot Dave Rask was about ten minutes out of Sentani in the big Caravan plane when his engine failed. He called May Day. He had just completed intensive training on the procedure to deal with engine failure. Following the guidelines, he shut down the motor and then tried starting it up again. It started, but without power. Flying over some pasture land, he glided into a grassy field. He landed, nose down, and flipped onto the wing. Both he and his passenger were fine. It was another miracle of divine protection.

• During a Women's Seminar, led by Anne Hobbs from Java, Indonesia, Elfrieda became aware that not everyone had the same tolerance for flying.

"Anne has been afraid of flying and dreamed almost every night that the plane was going to crash. Then I had a dream. I saw God's big hands above and below and even inside our little MAF airplane, all the way from Pyramid to Mapnduma. What a comfort to know that we do not have to fear!

When the time came for the next Marriage Seminar, Adriaan with Bill and Janet Kuhns flew in the first plane, while George and Anne Hobbs and I took the next one. George sat in front with the pilot. Anne and Meme, my language helper, and her baby were in the middle. Meme's husband and I sat in the back.

It was a clear day. As we started through the pass with the spiny ridge of mountains towering above us, that little plane was tossed up and down in the worst turbulence I had ever encountered. Meme was petrified. Anne was afraid, but when she saw how frightened Meme was, she put her arm around her to comfort her. As she did so, Anne's fear left.

God was answering my prayer for his peace and protection to surround the plane and resisting any evil forces that might be at work. His big, protecting hands sheltered us and landed us safely."

Airstrip Maintenance

One of Adriaan's responsibilities was the maintenance and construction of airstrips. He recognized the value and convenience of building new strips, which assisted in ministering to otherwise seldom-reached outposts. The people were thrilled and spiritually revitalized when Adriaan came with Nduga pastors to minister in their village churches. Children would flock into the church for children's meetings which were always fruitful with many first-time decisions and rededications to the Lord. His visit reenergized the literacy work, and many wanted Nduga Bibles sent to them. He was thankful for airstrips that opened the door for him to reach into the remote villages.

When Adriaan received word that the Mbuwa airstrip was ready for landing, he trekked a day's journey over the mountains to the Mugi Valley and overnighted there. The next morning, he went on to the Yigi Valley, slept there and climbed over more mountains into the Mbuwa. There he inspected the airstrip to find that it was not ready. For three full days, he helped the people work on it. The strip was still not long or wide enough. He left instructions before trekking back to Mapnduma. A few weeks later, he trekked in again, over the long trail, to check the condition of the airstrip. This time it was ready to be used.

> "More airstrips were needed to reach the entire tribe satisfactorily. The Keneyam strip in the lowlands, at only 400 feet above sea level, and the Jigi strip in the high mountains at 5,700 feet, was opened. Another airstrip, currently under construction in the Wosak Valley, will be a big help in the coming years since the terrain is so rough."

As the Ndugas became conversant with the ways of the outside world, they became more insistent on having their own airstrips. At times Adriaan tried to slow progress by reminding the Ndugas of their responsibilities. He could see that the appetite for more was insatiable, but the people did not understand the costs of the service. There was no doubt that air travel had transformed their ministry.

In 1984 the people of the Wosak had started to make a clearing in the jungles in the lowlands at a place called Nggeyarek.

> "We visited this place by helicopter. It will take a lot of work and patience to hack out an airstrip, but the site seems well located and suitable for it."

In reaching out to other villages, several strips are already functional. The Mbuwa, Wandama, Keneyam and Jigi strips are critical and strategic. Adriaan included his responsibilities with the various airstrips in his 1987 report:

"On September 14, the MAF helicopter flew me to the Mbuwa to upgrade the airstrip. While I was there, I also had the opportunity to assist the pastors in baptizing many candidates who had been discipled and were prepared to follow the Lord in baptism. I was encouraged that everyone seemed eager to listen to and obey God's Word.

I learned about a humorous incident from the first baptismal service in the Mbuwa I had participated in fourteen years earlier. An older man insisted on being the first candidate to step into the water. He told the others, 'I will be the first and if I drown you all run. If I come up alive, you all follow.' They all followed. God turned fear into a victory for many new believers. He is building his church, and many are now firmly fixed on the solid rock, Christ Jesus.

A few days later, I flew by helicopter to repair the airstrip at Yigi. Two airstrips in the lowlands needed repair, but I had to trek several days to get to them. We need to check out four new airstrips that are currently under construction in our areas. I could see that using the helicopter would be the primary mode of transportation in the future."

The work was constant and, at times, overwhelming.

"After I returned to Mapnduma, I continued to supervise the condition and construction of airstrips. I had recently opened an airstrip site at Alama, a very remote village west of Mapnduma. The people had not had a missionary visit since I had walked through there twenty-four years earlier on my way to Mapnduma for the first time. Now with the airstrip in operation, they were more connected.

I stayed in Mapnduma last week and visited Jita, a very hot and muggy outstation on the south coast. We built a big airstrip there, so it will be accessible by air, although almost an hour's flight away from Mapnduma. It is not ready for landing, and everyone is waiting for government permission to start using it. The airstrips at Yigi, Mbuwa, and Mapnduma all need repair work.

MAF has more and more regulations for the strips with all kinds of signs and measured markers."

The Rotor

Monday, December 23, 1992, a helicopter flight was scheduled to bring in a guest for Christmas because a pilot wasn't available for the plane. Adriaan was going to do some outstation work while the helicopter was at hand. As he was getting into the helicopter, he noticed some nationals standing in the take-off area. He motioned for them to move. As he did so, his left hand came in contact with the helicopter rotor blade.

Elfrieda saw Adriaan slump to the ground in pain. In an instant, she was at his side. She noticed his first two fingers were severed to the tendon and quickly assisted him to the house. At the house, Elfrieda almost lost control emotionally as she tried to splint the fingers. They needed help and every minute counted.

Elfrieda's sister, Elsie, visiting at the time, describes the reaction.

> "Preparations were made to see a doctor, and soon we were left waving at the departing helicopter. People were crying and praying. Everyone was in a state of shock. We picked up the pieces and tried to get a few things done at the house while we had our ear tuned to the radio."

After an hour in the air, the helicopter landed right in front of Mulia Mission Hospital. Dr. Jerry Powell came running out, wondering what had happened. When he learned of Adriaan's mishap, he took him under his arm and led him right into the operating room. Adriaan asked if his fingers could be saved, but it was not possible. When pilot Mike Brooks dropped in for a visit and prayer he encouraged Adriaan by saying, "We thank the Lord that you still have two hands to lift in praise to God." That turned Adriaan's sorrow into a renewed focus on God's faithfulness despite his loss.

After Adriaan's accident, he expected that he would soon be back into ministry. However, his arm began to atrophy after losing the two fingers. The doctors were concerned about nerve damage and sent him to Canada for medical evaluation. The neurosurgeon said it was disuse atrophy. The occupational therapist measured his left handgrip strength at eight pounds, while his other hand had seventy-eight pounds of strength. With therapy, it increased to forty-eight pounds. As Adriaan recounts his life, sitting around his dining table in Canada, there are still visible scars. He wears the missing fingers as a badge of honour now. When he raises his hands in worship, people recognize him as the missionary minus two fingers.

Phantom of the Jungle

The danger of flying children and families in and out of jungle airstrips hit home with a thud during Christmas 1968 in Sentani. No account tells it better than the eyewitness account of a ten-year-old survivor. Adriaan narrates the story.

> "The first tragedy hit on December 30, 1968, when one of our missionaries, Vida Troutman, died, possibly from cerebral malaria. We were shocked. Many of us went to her burial the next day. Because of the bad weather, we had to stay in Enarotali overnight.
>
> While we were attending Vida's burial, another crisis was developing. A small MAF aircraft was trying to find its way to Sentani with the Gene Newman family on board as they returned from their vacation on the south coast. The weather was so bad that the mountain tops were invisible. Pilot Menno Voth called Wamena and asked about the weather there. He got several suggestions on where to go, but there was no reply.
>
> When we heard about the crisis, everybody was tense. A search party was put together, and several men were asked to be ready early the next morning to do aerial searches for the lost plane.
>
> It was still quite dark when we left the next morning. Soon several planes were searching the area where they believed the plane had flown the day before. I was in a plane that flew over the Seng Valley. As we flew, the pilot told us about two missionaries who had been travelling in that valley just three months before. He pointed out several places where they slept and then, the place where they were killed. With thoughts of their deaths in our minds, we continued to watch the valley below us.
>
> As we flew lower and lower between the ranges in the same

area where the recent event had occurred, we began to see debris below us. We recognized it as the plane for which we were searching.

The pilot radioed Wamena indicating that the wreck seemed broken up with no signs of life. It looked like a fire had engulfed it and that no one could have survived, including the pilot, Gene and Lois Newman, their three sons, aged ten, five and one and a three-year-old daughter.

A helicopter was called in, but by the time it arrived, it was too late to land at the crash site. We went through a long night of waiting and wondering.

The next day the helicopter made a cautious approach, not knowing how the nearby people would respond. On board were axes and other items to pay the villagers to release any bodies we might find. When they landed, the crew saw that not much could be done. The plane and its contents had been destroyed.

They heard a scream from the other side of the valley. Ten-year-old Paul Newman stepped from the jungle undergrowth like a phantom. He came running to the crew. When they examined him, he did not have a scratch on him. It seemed impossible.

Paul told the crew what had happened. "We flew into the wrong valley. The pilot tried to turn around, but the valley had become too narrow, and the clouds came down like a blanket. In the last moments, we all understood that nothing could be done. One wing touched a tree, and we began to fall down the ridge. When my father tried to open the door, my little brother and sister flew out of the plane. When the plane stopped moving, everybody was dead. The plane had broken in two. There was not much time to escape, because fire had started. I crawled out. Otherwise, it might have been too late for me too! I could see a bridge nearby and knew that I could get to the village."

Paul did not know that these were the same villagers who had killed two missionaries who had come into the area three months earlier. One of the village men came to help him. The people gave him sweet potatoes to eat and kept him near the fire throughout the night to keep him warm. He slept a disconsolate night alone in the village. The crew was amazed that Paul had survived. Adriaan notes that another miracle, perhaps even greater, was the response of the people. They were friendly to the crew. They said, through an interpreter, that they were now ready to listen to what the missionaries had to say and that they would build an airstrip.

Don Richardson, in his book *Lords of the Earth*, relates that indeed God worked a transformation in their darkened hearts. In 1974 Phyliss Masters, the wife of one of the missionaries who was martyred there three months before, trekked into the village. She went in to see for herself the change God had wrought in the hearts of those who had slain her husband. Together, on the wing of the airplane, Phyllis partook of communion with the people who had killed her husband. It is truly a story of how God turned tragedy into triumph.

Not all mishaps ended in calamity, but this trauma reminded everyone that their lives were hanging by a thread most of the time, at the whim of the weather, mechanical failure, and pilot error. As MAF pilot Clell Rogers often said, "We cheated death again." Life is short and filled with swift transitions. We are here today and gone tomorrow. James 4:14 tells us: Your life is like the morning fog—here a little while and then it's gone. God has all our days here on earth already numbered. Lord, teach us to number each of our days so that we may grow in wisdom.

The log book of Adriaan and Mijo and Mary and Elfrieda's flying hours would fill several books. God has kept them in the hollow of his hand in every flight throughout the years.

15

WARS IN THE VALLEY

ONE OF THE CONSTANTS in Adriaan's life was acting as an intermediary in local wars. Beyond the messiness of settling old scores, Adriaan was more concerned that the warfare mentality stunted growth in the church when people were consumed with fighting.

The warring spirit of the Ndugas bred through centuries of clan and tribal conflict was quick to spill over at the drop of a hat, or perhaps we should say at the drop of a headdress. At the slightest provocation, they were ready for a tussle.

When Adriaan witnessed the coming together of the Wosak and the Kora groups in 1972, he recalled that they had once eaten their victims and turned their skulls into drinking containers. After releasing their anger and outrage toward those who were their enemies in the past, they had come together in a robust demonstration of unity, declaring that the gospel had made them one. With the cannibalistic lifestyle so prevalent, Adriaan recognized that only God could change a heart. Men from the Wosak and Kora groups would have to come for Bible School training at Mapnduma. God was building his church, and all the glory goes to him.

Mijo and Adriaan had travelled into the Jigi and Mbuwa Valleys in 1985. The Jigi Valley was still under the influence of a war that had raged there for the past two years, and people were edgy and careful not to cross over the boundaries.

"Along with the police and with God's guidance, I wanted to try to settle the war. However, the people did not want to listen. We made it clear to them that the consequences would include stopping all air traffic. Since then, we have heard of violent murders, so it seems that some people have turned away from the Lord."

The weariness of constant bickering that spilled over into war at the slightest provocation drained him.

"Forgiveness seems to be an unknown word to them. Revenge is the only code by which the carnal people live. There is no end to the war, only times of uneasy calm. The sad thing is that some of the preachers are directly or indirectly involved and have lost their credibility with the believers. The strong, faithful pastors and medical workers and school teachers stood for peace and did everything in their power to persuade the warring factions to lay down their weapons. Only the moving of God's Holy Spirit will bring these people to repentance and love for one another."

Rioters Arrive

Rioters came to the Wosak Valley and deceived the people, saying they were representatives of the Wamena police, so the Wosak people should give them pigs and the money from the church. They promised them high office jobs in a big city they were going to build. Being so isolated, the Wosak people believed it and had big feasts, with no questions asked. Then another group came from the Baliem Valley and countermanded the offer. The poor people were told to leave their faith, take second wives, and live as they used to.

Then a faithful elder, emboldened by the Spirit of the living God rose to his feet. Facing the group of men, he pointed to the church cross and proclaimed, "I believe in what the cross of Christ represents to us. Jesus came to die, shed his blood for us, and rose again. He won the victory over the devil. After all, he did for us we will not turn our back on him. Now in the name of the Lord Jesus Christ, leave." With that, the group turned on their heels and left. The Holy Spirit convicted them and rendered them powerless to proceed with their immoral plans. The van der Bijls rejoiced that the believers were not ashamed of the gospel. It is the power of God for salvation to all who believe.

The Seven-Year War

A full-scale war was not an everyday occurrence, but some ongoing feuds lasted for years. The legendary seven-year war was finally over in the Jigi Valley and solemnized with a large feast. In many ways, 1993 was a watershed year for the valleys of the highlands. Adriaan lived to enjoy the fruits of his labours and was able to answer the rhetorical question, Is there any doubt it was worth it? with a resounding yes. In Psalm 127 the Psalmist says: Unless the Lord builds the house, those who build it labour in vain.

While they were in Jigi, there was a celebration with more than fifty pit-cooked pigs, and then the two-way radio was officially turned over to the Jigi people. They gave a complete history of happenings since the gospel arrived, including their seven-year war. According to God's command, they decided to choose a peaceful lifestyle that it might go well with them and their children.

A Local Feud

It did not take long after the newlyweds Adriaan and Elfrieda returned to Mapnduma for a feud to erupt. There was the culturally-mandated pig feast, but soon afterward chaos erupted.

> "Everyone was running all over and chasing each other with weapons. Elsie was in the middle of it. When a man came running toward her with his weapons, she said BOO. The warrior turned on his heels and fled. Then the stones started flying, aimed at our houseboy's house. Someone had owed someone else a pig and had run into the houseboy's house for shelter. I had to stop it.
>
> The houseboy got into the fight, and then took shelter in our house. People came to our house, yelling at the top of their lungs."

All Elfrieda could think of to calm the frightened houseboy was the story of Jehoshaphat from 2 Chronicles 20 and how praise was used as a weapon to win the battle and send the devil on the run. She went upstairs and audibly started praising the Lord at the top of her lungs. The houseboy who was downstairs also started praising God. He must have been either scared or desperate but proved that praise dispels the darkness.

"After haranguing for some time, the guy left. Praising the Lord is a weapon that sends the devil away."

Personality Clash

A Bible School couple was a prime example in a class of forty-one couples who received help with their marriages during an in-service teaching week. At the end of one upgrading school for these pastors, Elfrieda reported that the training had netted important results.

"Among them are men like Musa, our local pastor, who graduated some ten years ago. While in Bible School, he had a hard time with his marriage. A clash surfaced during Bible School days, resulting in a one-year suspension. That year brought significant maturing. Musa persevered, re-entered Bible School, graduated, and has had an outstanding and effective pastoral ministry. It was during the hostage crisis that Musa, like Moses in the Bible, went up the mountain and called on God: "Lord, please bring my people back from the jungle."

One early morning God rewarded him with a miraculous display of heavenly splendour. In amazement, he witnessed a dazzling light slowly moving up from the east and at the same time a brilliant red light coming up from the west and amalgamating over Mapnduma. Musa knew God was telling him he was in charge and would not leave them.

While Musa was serving in the Iniye Valley, a local feud broke out over an adultery case. A man was killed, and against Musa's advice, many participated in the battle. Musa's brother-in-law, Yoram, became a victim of the riot, paralyzed from the waist down because of an arrow wound.

After Musa became the pastor at Mapnduma, Yoram became very ill. Musa walked several days over rugged terrain to see him. As Yoram lay dying, he spoke these words: "The angels are coming for me. I'm going! Please do not take revenge. Tell the people not to kill someone over my death. Do not kill pigs for retaliation. I am going to heaven."

Then Yoram put his New Testament under his right arm and the Old Testament on his chest and asked Musa to read the Psalms to him. By the light of his flashlight, Musa read throughout the night until the batteries died. Yoram's dying words were, "Look at the angels. They are waiting for me." He escaped earth for his eternal reward.

The account indicates how the people struggled to restore broken relationships and live in peace. The story of Musa and Yoram demonstrates the positive hope the Ndugas have in following the Lord.

16

PEACE IN THE VALLEY

WHILE LIFE IN PAPUA WAS A ROUTINE OF ACTIVITY, there was occasional space for slowing down. Those freeze-frame moments stuck in Adriaan's mind like slices cut out of time itself. Among the moments he treasured were times spent with Mijo. They were too few, and too distant, as were those cherished windows of opportunity to be with his children. In time, Elfrieda would become part of that tapestry.

Adriaan did not stop long enough for many reflections unless he was writing a report or sending out a prayer letter. Between the lines of his busy workload, we gather glimpses of a man who cherished those special moments.

> "Relaxing picnics were impromptu and makeshift. A patch of grass or rock often became an excuse for family downtime that triggered lifetime memories. Another highlight, while we were in Penang, Malaysia, was the opportunity to baptize Paul. I recalled the baptisms of my other children: Daniel in Holland, David in the little church in Erie, and Heidi in the swimming pool at the WLD Ranch."

A Surprise and Birthday Parties

One quiet evening, Adriaan's youngest son, Paul trekked to Mapnduma from Wamena, a five to six-day trek over rugged high ranges to surprise them before he left to attend Moody Bible Institute in Chicago, Illinois, USA. They saw him coming down the trail near their home. He looked like a mud baby after the trek over the mountains and through the valleys during the rainy weather season. After the shock wore off, they settled in for a welcomed visit. Moments like this were rare. Receiving a family member trekking over the mountains was singular. They maximized the time, and it goes down in Adriaan's memory bank as very near the top of the list.

Making the most of special occasions was not as easy as picking up a birthday cake at the local supermarket. Elfrieda had been thinking about how she could give Adriaan a birthday meal. She had mentioned to Sakius that she wanted to buy a chicken for Adriaan's birthday. He checked with his young twin boys, Seid and Yiben, to see if one of them would like to give up his chicken, but no bird was forthcoming.

> "I didn't hear anything about it for the rest of the day, so I began to develop plan B. On the morning of his birthday, Adriaan came in to tell me that Yiben had brought his chicken, and the whole family was out there waiting for me. I hurried out and saw Yiben holding a big chicken for me.

I offered to pay, but they didn't want anything. Since they usually prefer a trade, I gave them a can of mackerel, some noodle
packages with spices, candy, gum and some cookies. It will add a
bit of variety to their customary mealtime of sweet potatoes morning, noon and night.

That was the perfect birthday meal. The chicken was not the
usual, tough and hard-to-chew kind, but deliciously tender. We had
completed our dinner of fried chicken, crisped potatoes, Harvard
beets, copper pennies, squash casserole, lime jellied salad and cran-
berries and were ready for the dessert when there was a tap on the
door. There was Sakius. He added a lot of fun to the party with his
usually funny comments that had us doubled over with laughter."

Elfrieda was single for a good chunk of her life. It made her especially aware
of the joy of having a husband to share her special days. He was an attentive
man and often surprised her with unique memories. While attending a seminar on overseeing orphanages and helping with disadvantaged regions hosted by the Bishop of the Protestant Church in Bali, Indonesia, Elfrieda writes:

"For my fiftieth birthday, Adriaan gave me some beautiful
Indonesian gold earrings. At coffee break, the Bishop announced
my birthday and they surprised me with a lovely birthday cake
and fresh bouquet of orchids that Adriaan had ordered. In the evening they performed an incredible outdoor Balinese dance with
music. It was amazing."

Adriaan's sixtieth was a special time of celebration. Pilot Rick Willms
brought in Myrna Maxey and her son Benny. They all enjoyed the coffee and
the cake Myrna had made to celebrate. Adriaan shared his testimony of sixty
years with the Lord. After the surprise birthday celebration, the visitors flew
back to Wamena. For supper, Elfrieda prepared a special fondue meal. For
Adriaan, it was a treat. It was like a pre-Christmas celebration.

Smelling the Roses

By 1991, it became apparent to both Adriaan and Elfrieda that they needed
regular recovery time.

"We decided that we would take some time off. In July we went to Bali, with our sisters Elsie, Elviera, and son Paul. We had a most wonderful relaxing time. It was delightful to laze around on the Bali beach and do some shopping. Our time was topped off with a boat trip to Sumatra where we toured my childhood home, including the Japanese internment sites.

On another trip to Bandung, Java with Elsie and Elviera, we hired a driver to take us on an excursion to Mount Tangkuban Perahu, an active volcano that resembles an overturned boat. This is a crater that people have viewed with awe since ancient times. Our guide told us that the rocks were hot enough to fry an egg. We believed him as we watched the hot lava bubbling at the bottom of the crater. Steam from the intense heat formed clouds as it escaped from the gigantic cavity. It was fascinating."

Christmas in Mapnduma

Christmas was always a time for throwbacks as Adriaan rehearsed special times like their first Christmas in Mapnduma as a family when Mijo came in with their three children, and they lived in a tent set up in the large round-house-style church for their first three weeks. As an extraordinary Christmas gift, Adriaan had their two-story rustic house ready to move in on Christmas Eve.

Another special memory was celebrating his thirty-ninth birthday in November 1968 and then having friends join them for Christmas.

> "The Teeuwens, Jacques, a fellow Dutchman, and his charming wife Ruth, came from Karubaga to celebrate Christmas with us. It was an inspiring time to celebrate the birth of Jesus Christ together with our special friends. It was also a time of reflection and sharing the lessons that life brings and learning from each other. They became some of our best friends."

In the Center of their God-Given Destiny

And in the moments when pressures subsided, Adriaan and Elfrieda had those epiphany flashes that confirmed that they were in the right place and were living fully in the center of their God-given destiny. In a letter home, Elfrieda describes one of those rare windows into why they were so at peace in the valley.

> "With the rain beating on the aluminum roof just above me, it is hard to imagine that you are about to enjoy a white Christmas. I am wondering if it is frosty cold or just a lovely hoar-frost winter wonderland in Canada. Just an hour ago, at six p.m. Adriaan and I observed a most breathtaking sunset. The whole sky was orange. It was like looking at the world through stained sunglasses as pink-tinted clouds billowed up, framed by the southern mountains. We were overwhelmed with God's creative wonders as were our Nduga friends here. Suddenly a flash of lightning melted into the sky. Wow!"

The task of writing a Christmas letter as the season approached jogged her back to reality.

> "Well, as you are busy with your last-minute shopping, we are landlocked at Mapnduma, with no stores. But upstairs, in our

storage room, is a trunk with a few Christmas gifts which we sorted through and chose for the pilot friends we will likely visit while on vacation at Bokondini for Christmas this year. We are looking forward to spending a relaxing Christmas with Elsie and several other teacher friends from the coast."

They had learned to make do with much less than they knew others were enjoying, as well as the absence of family at this festive time of the year. They did not chafe at their lot but made the best of every occasion to bless and encourage others. And when they could, to their last year in Papua, they learned that the rhythm of life included rest.

As with work, they had learned the value of play. A mentor colleague had said, "Remember, wherever you are, be all there." Adriaan and Elfrieda embraced the mantra right through to their final year in Papua.

Final homecoming was not on the horizon. For now, an occasional evening by the fireplace was enjoyable and made a cheery substitute.

17

THE CHURCH THAT REMAINS

SUCCESS AND ACCOMPLISHMENT after thirty-five years of Christian presence in a remote outpost of civilization could not be quantified in gains or losses, as much as in the lives of selected individuals who continued on after Adriaan and Elfrieda were gone.

Historical perspective is essential to measure the impact and lasting results of anything. Many times, in telling his story, Adriaan insisted that this story was bigger than him. It was about the God to whom we must give the glory for orchestrating the entrance of the Nduga people into the Kingdom of God.

Near the end of Adriaan's active career, he sought to summarize what had happened over the years. In a 1991 report, he noted that pastoral training was slowing down. The valleys were blessed with many pastors.

> "Throughout the years God directed more than one hundred preachers and evangelists to be trained in our Sion Bible School. The availability of the New Testament, faithfully translated into Nduga by Mary Owen Byrne, has strengthened pastoral training.

Children's ministries have blossomed under the godly and dedicated leadership of Niko and Gideon and many others as taught and mentored by Elfrieda.

New workers were trained in several valleys resulting in hundreds of children now being taught and nurtured in the Word. Leadership was in the hands of many strong and dedicated Nduga leaders. Godly public school teachers had made an impact in the lives of children now going on to higher education in other areas.

At the Jigi Annual Church Conference May 20–24, 1991 two districts changed their District Superintendent leadership with a smooth transition."

He noted the need to pray for Sakius, one of the new District Superintendents, as he undertakes supervision and leadership of the Mapnduma district and as well as Monggat in the Mbuwa district. As usual, the Church Conference decisions were sealed with a dedication service followed by a massive pig feast.

"Over 1,000 people gathered daily for fellowship and feasting in the Word and a huge celebration with over 200 pigs in the pits."

In 1992 Adriaan was able to report that while they were away on medical leave, the Nduga Shorter Version of the Old Testament had arrived. It will enhance the pastoral upgrading seminar for Nduga pastors in the Mbuwa scheduled to begin in October.

Dissonant Chords

The festering presence of false prophets among the Ndugas was beginning to show its true colours. The unsettling first signs began to surface in August of 1992. The heresy was gaining traction in a hurry, and by October Adriaan knew it was serious.

"We got our eyes opened a bit more as to what is going on in this false prophet cult. They tell many lies as they go about affecting other areas. Satan is still the father of lies. One pastor came to us yesterday so distraught, not knowing what to do in his village. Youth by the scores are led astray."

There was a premature announcement that the threat had peaked but it was only momentary.

> "They claim to be visited by the spirits of the dead. The spirit will enter someone who seeks to be possessed and then speaks through that one in the deceased one's voice. They kill pigs and dance to become possessed.
>
> The movement began with one man in our next valley, who accused three women of being witches involved in the death of an elder who died when his house burned. The possessed man spread it to another valley, and since then it has become an epidemic, with some pastors becoming involved. It is devilish. They accuse innocent people of breaking their connection with Satan if they pass over the devil's cord and then demand payment for it."

Kick Back from the Powers

Adriaan had seen substantial growth and maturity in the church.

> "We are in the second week of teaching in our Pastoral Upgrading School in the Mbuwa. We are thrilled with sixty-eight enthusiastic pastors from village churches. Every Friday they go to seventeen churches in the Mbuwa Valley and over the mountain to the Jigi Valley with the gospel. They are all fired up, expecting great things."

People were so excited about what God was doing that everyone wanted to share about their weekend experience. Elfrieda remembers that we did not have time for everyone to report the weekend's happenings.

The following Sunday, back in Mapnduma, Elfrieda had more details about the situation with the false cult.

> "Yesterday the Christian leaders met with us to discuss what stand they should take against the enemy's workings in our midst."

As a church, they made some concrete decisions for combating the cult. They would inform those involved in the false cult not to visit the Christians' homes to propagate their evil intentions. Christians were warned and forbidden from paying money to the cult if they should happen to come by and forcefully demand money. They were to remind the cult members that any powers that had connected them to the enemy had been unplugged and to declare that the power cord has been broken.

> "This was a Sunday where we had to prove whose authority we stood on, and it stood the test. During this past Communion Sunday, there were no disturbances in church. Adriaan preached a powerful message against the falsity of the false prophets that will arise in the last days."

The demonic teaching influenced even the children. While Adriaan was preaching to the adults, Elfrieda broached the matter with the children.

> "Eighteen children made first-time decisions, and twelve stayed to repent of their involvement in the false teachings. I was surprised at how small the children were who had gotten involved out of curiosity. One girl's whole body shook, so we prayed for her. She was delivered and set free. The children's desire to do the right thing opened the door to more discipleship and teaching with the children."

The discipleship and teaching of children was a continual blessing for Elfrieda in her ministry with Adriaan.

Adriaan Reflects on the Ndugaland Churches

Adriaan did not know as he headed into 1995 that it would be his last term of uninterrupted ministry in Mapnduma. Some of his journal entries and letters foreshadowed the future of the Nduga church. His role as Coordinator of Evangelism required him to travel and survey the growth of the Papuan church and churches in other parts of Indonesia.

> "Accompanied by my national counterpart, Peterus Done, we had seminars at two stations in the Wissel Lakes with 450 pastors and workers attending. The main thrust was reaching out to pockets of unreached tribes in Papua.
>
> In Haga, I stood at the grave of Kama Kama, the very first evangelist to the Nduga tribe at Mapnduma. His son is now an evangelist and translator. Then I visited the southern islands of Indonesia, Timor and Sumba, and recalled that Soe, capital of South Central Timor, was a centre of a revival in the 1960s.
>
> A weekend visit to Sumba culminated in a baptismal service in which I was asked to officiate followed by a mass wedding of seventeen couples."

Back in Papua, the van der Bijls had spent Christmas in hot, humid Timika which Adriaan described as an unplanned, overcrowded and dirty construction town on the south coast of Papua. Ever the consummate evangelist, Adriaan could not help but think of this unkempt city as a target for evangelism. The appeal of Timika for Adriaan was not its culture or comfort level. The appeal was always measured in terms of people who need the gospel message.

> "Opportunities in Timika are unlimited. We not only assist with the already seven or eight established tribal churches but can also reach out to the large community of people from other islands in Indonesia. Many are Muslim migrants from Java. There is a wide mixture of languages, cultural background and religious beliefs in this area."

The Advent season was observed with the introduction of the Advent wreath to a Sunday School gathering of tribal children. Adriaan allowed himself the luxury of revisiting the scene afterward in his mind. It was a vision that would sustain him in the difficult years ahead when he longed to be with the people he loved.

> "Imagine yourself in the midst of 130 dark-skinned, wide-eyed children and adults in a Christmas setting. Their enthusiastic singing makes the rafters quiver. Then the seven tribal church groups filed up separately to share a special song in their tribal languages. Excitement filled the church as we opened the first Sunday of Advent calendar and focused on the theme, Anticipation and Longing for the Coming of Jesus."

Adriaan savoured the moment as his thoughts turned to the hope of Christ's soon return and the realization that someday 130 dark-skinned, wide-eyed children and adults would join him around Christ's triumphant throne.

The Nduga Nation Comes of Age

The Papuan threads of independence were strong, and this played into the hands of the independence movement leaders. The cultural context of the independence revolution is perhaps best epitomized in the town of Tembagapura. Adriaan journaled in 1993 that they had travelled to Tembagapura for a weekend of ministry there.

"It is always amazing to us that located right there in the jungle, in a landscape very much the same as Mapnduma, is a typical American town. It now has more than 10,000 people and is still growing. There are plans for another town in the lowlands. This area has what is most likely the biggest copper mine in the world. It's a unique setting.

There are about 350 expats here. The rest are Indonesians of which about ten percent are Papuans. There are lots of tensions between the different groups, as well as a great difference between the lifestyle of the foreigners and the locals.

For instance, not many miles away, the Damal tribe lives, as they have always lived, in their humble little huts. Authorities are trying to improve their image among the tribal people by providing housing in the lowlands, but down there inundated by mosquitos that invade their huts, malaria kills them off by the dozens."

That disparity never ceased to trouble Adriaan and goad him to do all he could do to right the imbalance. It was good to get back to the Mbuwa in late 1995.

"As I write letters, I look out at the mountains shrouded in clouds. It gives me a restful feeling. After five months of hectic travel all over Indonesia, it was like coming to a complete stop. Not that we have nothing to do. In fact, it seemed that there was never enough time to do what we like to do, including writing letters.

We had a wonderful pastoral upgrading seminar in the Mbuwa in October and November. Around fifty pastors, wives, children and youth leaders and other church workers filled the youth center each day for upgrading and inspiration. Elfrieda taught the discipleship course, Following Jesus. Four weeks later, these church leaders took more than 200 books back to their isolated churches to help their fellow Ndugas toward spiritual maturity in Christ.

The responses from those who took the course, Following Jesus, were encouraging. Smiley's daughter said that she used to steal from him, but now she realizes that was wrong, and she has stopped. Another person remarked that the course had helped fix his intention on remaining true to the Lord."

18

HOSTAGES

On January 8, 1996, an event of monstrous consequence rocked Mapnduma. The repercussions were felt around the world. Four biologists from the United Kingdom had teamed with four Indonesian scientists to undertake an important study of flora and fauna of the Lorentz Nature Reserve which included the Nduga area. Rebel forces, representing the Liberation Movement Papua, seized the researchers a few weeks before their scheduled departure from Papua. Government authorities asked Adriaan to be part of the negotiation team charged with securing their release.

Some of the rebels were young boys when Adriaan first knifed his way through the undergrowth and located a landing strip on the edge of the mountain. Now they were using his airstrip and house to stage their version of a rebellion as they tried to gain independence from the Indonesian government.

As Adriaan was preparing for final celebratory closure to Mapnduma and thirty-five years of fruitful God-honouring ministry, a titanic struggle to save lives and negotiate complicated military intrigue exploded around him. It was not how he had envisioned his final years with the Ndugas.

The event is documented in detail in *The Open Cage: The Ordeal of the Irian Jaya Hostages*, the story of the tragedy told by the expedition leader, Daniel Start. [3]

> "It was in December 1995 that we first heard from Adriaan and Elfrieda van der Bijl, the resident missionaries in the Nduga region of Lorentz. These extraordinary people had lived in the Nduga area for over thirty years, and they told us about food, language, air transport, accommodation and, of course, the people themselves, with whom they had discussed our plans. As for safety, they said there would be no problems. With the assurance of the van der Bijls, and with all the advice I had gathered in Indonesia and Britain, I was confident that we had chosen a peaceful place to work." [4]

Daniel Start first met Elfrieda van der Bijl at the mission office in Wamena when he was preparing for their expedition. He remembered that she was looking rather windswept as she heaved a generator out of a Cessna onto a trolley. But she wiped the oil from her hand before she took mine."[5] His first impression of the couple was their obvious devotion to each other.

> "They had both returned to Wamena that morning from far-flung mission posts and had not seen each other for several weeks. Adriaan and Elfrieda embraced warmly. Looking down on me with his wise eyes and shining blond hair he had the air of a biblical figure. He was a tall, strong man in his late sixties, graceful and gentle in his manner but with a rugged look that spoke of many adventures." [6]

There is always value in the objective first-time experience of a culture and people. Start does a masterful job of capturing the learning curve of his expedition in their new setting beginning with his perceptions of Mapnduma.

---

[3] Daniel Start. The Open Cage. p. 35-36: The Ordeal of the Irian Jaya Hostages. Harper Collins Publishers: Hammersmith, London. 1997.

[4] p. 35.

[5] p. 35.

[6] p. 36.

"While most Nduga villages were just a handful of huts in the remote tropical rain forest, Mapnduma was a virtual metropolis.
It had tin-roofed houses, a small clinic, a church, a missionary
house, lots of Nduga-style huts, an airstrip and even a school with
an Indonesian flag on the pole. There was little forest, most having been stripped for cultivation to feed almost a thousand people
who had been attracted to the Nggul Valley in search of progress."[7]

The personal journey into self-awareness was fast-tracked for Start and his
team when they became captives. Daniel was quick to understand that they
were in a difficult situation and his biography gives credence to his fears.

"When I thought of dying now there was nothing but a cold, dark
loneliness. Living a good life in the real world was all I thought
about these days. After all, I was a young man with things to
prove and people to meet. I felt I had let something precious slip
away. I had neglected my faith and now I wanted it back more
than anything."[8]

What we can draw from his story is the understanding he began to have
of the Nduga church. He was aware that they were a conflicted group. Several
believers were drawn into the independence war and did not know how to
deal with the tension between their faith and their sense of national destiny.
Some were in the group that captured Start's team. Start referred to the depth
of their faith more than once. When recounting some of the characteristics of
the men taken hostage with them he singled out Sakius, Mapnduma's District
Superintendent, saying "He is a man who walks his talk."

"I was unsure how superstitious Silas or the Ndugas were. It was
their Christian beliefs they talked of most. Both days we had been
in Aptam Silas had come and prayed with us and told us that only
the Lord could decide what would happen now. Almost all the
men with us claimed to be Christians, and many spoke highly of
Adriaan van der Bijl as if he were the father figure of the Ndugas.

[7] p. 50.
[8] p. 111.

Some of the men told me they hoped Father van der Bijl would come and help them. They were confident he would know what to do." [9]

Adrian tried.

Adriaan's Account

"Since we were not living at Mapnduma for a while, we had made arrangements for a group on a scientific expedition in the Lorentz Nature Reserve to rent our house while they did research on the wildlife in the area. They had lived there for two months as they did their studies, developing good working relationships with the Ndugas.

On January 8, 1996, 300 members of the Liberation Movement Papua rushed into Mapnduma and took the twenty-six people hostage. Our church leaders tried to protect the team of researchers but were overwhelmed by the sheer force of this rebel group. In terror, many villagers fled into the jungle.

Fifteen Nduga hostages were released relatively quickly. However, the remaining twelve hostages—four Britons, five Indonesians, two Netherlanders and one German—remained in Free Papua Movement, Organisasi Papua Merdeka (OPM) hands while a network of people including the International Committee of the Red Cross (ICRC) tried to get them released. Martha Klein, one of the captives, was three months pregnant at the time.

The OPM rebels specifically requested that John Gobay, provincial head of the national church, the Catholic Bishop Monseigneur Munninghoff, and I, come in to negotiate.

On January 15, we went in for the first time from Wamena where we were staying with the Maxey family which was a healing balm for us. We spent four hours negotiating. The German hostage, Frank, was released to make the rebels' grievances known to the Indonesian authorities. Ten days later, Bishop Munninghoff met Kelly Kwalik, the Catholic leader of the rebellion and hostage-takers. Kwalik gave him a message for the ICRC, requesting that it act as a neutral humanitarian intermediary.

---

[9] p. 116.

Bishop Munninghoff contacted the British, Indonesian and Netherland governments, since the hostages were from these countries, asking for their consent to serve in this intermediary capacity. After obtaining their consent, the ICRC agreed to play this role.

Elfrieda and I went to Mapnduma on February 3 to reassure the people and encourage them to return from the jungle to which they had fled. We found that our house was ransacked and all that was left was rubble after it had been pilfered. We lost many precious things, and it was traumatic for both of us.

There were only men in the village when we arrived, but the women slowly came out from hiding in the jungle when they knew that we expected to stay. They returned to their homes to try to pick up a normal life again. We held a service the next Sunday and afterward handed out clothing and some food to the group of fifty that showed up.

We learned that, during the time that they were hiding in the jungle, many people were sick and five had died. One pastor, Josias, lost two of his children and was himself malnourished and weak after being sick for a long time. He is so weak that he can't concentrate enough to pray.

On February 7, a five-member negotiating team struggled through the dense jungle, high altitudes, bad weather and numerous other problems to contact Kwalik. At that point, they arranged for a meeting to be held on February 25.

I joined the negotiating team on four occasions, doing my best to negotiate an early release of the hostages. Finally, the military went in and occupied Mapnduma.

As time went on, it became quite clear that it would be better for Elfrieda and me to withdraw from Mapnduma. I was exhausted from the turmoil. We moved to Sentani February 21 and stayed with Elsie. It was a healing balm to be with her for a while. Mike Sohm, from C&MA headquarters, came in and ministered to us. We were advised not to move back to Mapnduma or even to the Mbuwa for the time being. So we decided, after staying for several weeks in Sentani, that we would go back to Timika.

We continued to be concerned about the hostage situation. Annoyance seemed to be building because there was no direct negotiation for the release of the hostages. The press was growing frustrated that they were not able to be on the spot. The hostages' families and associated organizations became increasingly irritated as they didn't seem to understand the degree of remoteness involved."

Adriaan knew the area and editorialized that Mapnduma is remote, but the hostages are held somewhere beyond that remoteness. Letters home signalled people to pray.

"In the midst of chaos and uncertainty, we were daily assured of the Lord's presence. We know he is Lord of all times, including the chaotic ones. The knowledge that people were praying kept us going. While we could grow weary in well-doing, we knew that the Lord had something to teach the Nduga people and us through all this.

The day the hostages were taken away to the forest the Nduga people saw a radiant light in the form of a shimmering cross, and a man in white precede the hostages into the jungle that first day.

This whole ordeal was trying. Pastor Musa at Mapnduma often went up the mountain nearby to pray. Just three days after the invasion, God sent a striking sign for the Ndugas to see. Just before sunrise on January 11, a fluttering sound filled the air, and then a dazzling light from the north appeared and began to rise over Mapnduma. At the same time, a red light appeared in the south. Both lights rose simultaneously, totally enveloping Mapnduma and merging overhead in the form of two hands. The light remained for over four hours. Everyone who gazed at the marvel in the sky knew that God was giving his angels charge over them and was surrounding them, like a capsule, with his shield during the terrifying days ahead."

All eleven hostages were present when the ICRC team arrived in Geselema for the meeting on February 25. A Red Cross doctor examined them and found that they were healthy, though most were reported to have become much thinner during their stay in the jungle.

Unrest began to occur in other areas. Another meeting between the ICRC and the hostage-takers was arranged for March 26-27. At that meeting, one of the two remaining Papuan hostages was handed over to the ICRC and immediately taken to Timika to join his family. Three other meetings followed on April 17, May 5, and 8—all in Geselema (several trekking days west of Mapnduma). No progress was being made.

On Wednesday, May 15, the Indonesian Army Special Forces encircled the area where the hostages were being held, hoping to effect their release. As the military was preparing to raid the site, the rebels acted. They grabbed Navy, an Indonesian. While Adina, his fiancée watched helplessly, he was slashed with a machete. As the OPM rebel kept chopping him to death, he called out, "Praise the Lord. I go to be with the Lord Jesus." The murderer then went after Yosias Matias, the Indonesian head of the science project, killing him. The remaining nine hostages fled to the helicopter pad where the military was waiting, screaming, "Don't shoot. We are the hostages." They were finally in safe hands.

Due to bad weather, the military was not able to get them out of the jungle until Thursday morning. They were all hospitalized for evaluation and treatment. Although they were thin due to the scarcity of food and some bad infections and skin disease, overall their condition was good. Martha Klein, despite her pregnancy, was in good condition.

"The hostages were turned over to their respective embassies on May 18. The military stated that they were going to chase down all the rebels. All we could do was pray that they would have wisdom and discern who needed to be arrested and who should not be so innocent people would not suffer. In a letter in which I described some of the events, I concluded:

This account is a short version of the beginning months of this year. What a year it already has been.

Papua sure has been in the news, with a major earthquake on February 17 in Biak, as well as a major outbreak of sickness in one of our Nduga valleys where more than one hundred people have died. All this has brought this island into world focus and prayer.

We believe the Lord has something special for the Papuan people, so let's keep on praying.

We are praying that we will keep our eyes riveted on the Lord because we could easily get discouraged and depressed. We have felt that many of you have held us up and we pray that we and especially our Nduga people and churches will come through victoriously. Psalm 103 is always a psalm of praise in times of difficulties."

View from The Captives' Cage

Insights into the spiritual psyche of Start's captors indicate that either they truly believed that the child of their captive, Martha Klein, would become their new saviour, or they had been fed this line by leaders higher up the chain. Their mixed-up beliefs indicate this.

> "We have waited many years and put our faith in the Lord to send a saviour to the people of West Papua. Now he has sent the second messiah, as it is written in the Bible. Martha's baby will be born on Papuan soil, and it will be called Papuani, for a girl, or Papuana for a boy. The messiah will come, and West Papua will be free!" [10]

During the captivity, Kelly Kwalik, one of the OPM ringleaders, and a companion met with the captors. Kwalik's companion began to rant about their cause. The name Bethlehem always appeared on the papers the captors were asked to sign. When Start asked about the meaning of the word Bethlehem on the paper, he was in for a tirade of venom.

> "Why, have you never read the Bible?" the man snapped indignantly. "Bethlehem was the birth place of Jesus Christ. He was born here in Papua, and now the Lord has sent his successor. Martha will bear the child, and Papua will be free." He straightened his heavy cross, and he and Kwalik stood up."[11]

During their captivity, Daniel Start and his fellow captives moved from serenity to boredom to desperation as they tried to make sense of it all.

---

[10] p. 135.
[11] p. 153.

"So little linked me to home, so much had been taken away, so uncertain was the future and yet, despite all these things, I felt supremely content. It was as if adversity had freed me of my bonds and allowed me to live for just that moment." [12]

As the days wore on, he began to see the work differently. "I searched the skies for the familiar pattern of the Plough or Orion's Belt but realized that from this place on earth even my view of the universe had changed." He flirted with the sense of freedom that living with nothing gave him. "With poverty came an extraordinary feeling of liberty.... There was nothing to pack, nothing to be stolen, nothing to worry about. I was as poor as a Papuan." [13]

"In every day there are beautiful things. One must find them and live with them." [14]

In the end, he was drawn to the spiritual grounding of men like Philipus and Petrus. [15]

"We linked hands, and Philipus prayed for the plight of everyone trapped between the army and the rebels. Petrus prayed loudly at least three times every night. His rambling Indonesian monologues asked the Lord to protect the hostages, and he always tried to list all our names but missed some and repeated others."

Daniel became aware of the spiritual drama that was undergirding their situation: "The world in which we were captive did not pay heed to sense or reason." [17]

There were omens, superstitions, emotions, dreams that only the spirits understood. As time dragged on, the hostages adopted varying coping mechanisms to survive. For Daniel Start, the only way to handle it was to give in to the possibility that he might never get out.

---

[12] p. 173.

[13] p. 199.

[14] p. 153.

[15] Start described Petrus as "our affectionate and loyal helper."

[16] p. 213.

[17] p. 241.

"I had always wanted to live in a forest, perhaps one just like this. If only I could forget that I was a prisoner, perhaps I could find pleasure in life again. I had grown strong with the determination to live with joy and passion no matter what the circumstances."

For Daniel Start and his fellow hostages, the release was the beginning of a long process of grief and rebuilding. Most of them had survived an unimaginable circumstance.

We are indebted to Daniel for chronicling what they endured with such precision and perception. For Adriaan and Elfrieda, who were unwilling spectators in the drama, the cost was perhaps as high as for the young men and women held captive. Mapnduma had become their world. They were virtual pawns when for years they had been the players.

19

THE TAPESTRY UNFOLDS

AFTER A SIX-MONTH FURLOUGH to recover after the hostage crisis events, Adriaan and Elfrieda returned in 1997 for their final two years in Papua. There was hope for a satisfactory concluding chapter, but it was not to be.

Hit by Drought

> "We are facing unforeseen disasters. The drought had hit hard. The sweet potatoes that the Ndugas have always relied on as their main food are now finger thin and shrivelled up in the ground."

Adriaan and Elfrieda were again flying over Ndugaland. They received permission to use the MAF helicopter to survey four out of the twelve major Nduga valleys. The aerial view indicated that fires had destroyed large areas of forest and scarred many gardens. Food was scarce, resistance was low, and sickness was increasing. It was heartbreaking for the van der Bijls. Yet nothing they saw prepared them for what they would face when they landed.

"As we stepped out of the helicopter, the physical condition of the men, women and children glared us in the face. Many children, with every rib visible, had yellow hair, an obvious sign that their nutritional state is critical. Upper arm circumference measurement confirmed sixty-five percent severe malnutrition among children under five at this village due to the drought."

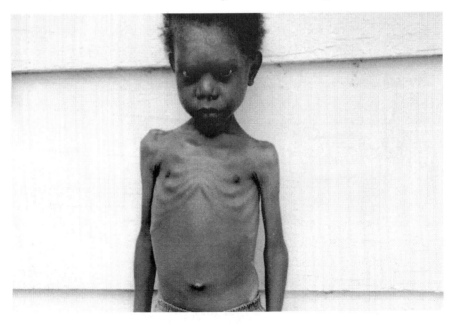

Even in the Baliem, gardens were drying out. To add to this, it had been unbearably cold in the highlands with freezing temperatures at 9,000 feet altitude, destroying many gardens.

> "We are sleeping under three blankets and a hot water bottle these days and are so grateful for a cozy fireplace which we fire up early in the morning and most evenings."

As the year progressed, the El Niño weather pattern continued to affect millions in Asia and the world. The haze engulfed Jakarta and much of Java where new fires were now burning. On October 31, MAF announced that they would only be doing flights to provide relief in the coming months. As the drought continued, thick smog hampered needed flights.

> "Several villages were without food. We needed a miracle. When we think of the isolation of our Nduga areas geographically, it makes us feel weak. With the thick smog and no planes moving, it would take a miracle."

On November 12, Adriaan wrote:

> "The devastating drought that has wreaked havoc in most of this island has eased somewhat, but the sweet potato vines have dried in the ground which will leave thousands of highlanders hungry."

Adriaan felt each pain and suffering of the Nduga people as if it were his own. But miracles came.

> "Just thought you would like to hear what God did in the Jigi Valley, a six-hour walk over the mountain from us here in the Mbuwa. Their potatoes had shrivelled up. On September 26, a helicopter came in with a load of sweet potatoes, five sacks of rice and two boxes of dried fish. The people rallied and decided to cook the potatoes in their separate villages.
>
> While the potatoes were steaming in the pits, the people at Pastor Niko's village church in Yal gathered to pray. Niko

reminded them what God did when the children of Israel ran out of food and water. With that reminder, they called on God for rain. Suddenly we heard the sound of raindrops hitting the aluminum roof. Then the heavens opened, the rains came down, and the floods came up.

The stream beds began to fill up, and bridges were washed out. The dry, cracked land welcomed the cloudburst. What a miracle. People's hearts melted. One man, who had not darkened the door of the church for years, said that he had never seen God answer prayer in such a miraculous way. He was now a believer."

Then in March 1998, Mapnduma suffered extensive landslides. In this, God enabled Adriaan to arrange for rice and oil to be distributed to the hard-hit areas. Sakius stepped up and intervened on behalf of affected families.

"District Superintendent Sakius bravely entered the bombed hostage area of Nggeselema a month ago and moved several families out of the forest to Mapnduma. Then, when their gardens were destroyed in landslides last week, the families moved back to Nggeselema. Now Sakius and his committee plan to open a new area at Paru Paru south of Mapnduma. It would be free of landslides and provide an area for the Nduga people to live that is not constantly under suspicion of rebels, as Nggeselema is. God has blessed this move and enabled a large airstrip to be opened which has served the people well."

The fruit of national leaders trained by Adriaan and the missionary team was having an effect. On another front, Elfrieda's work was also having an impact.

"April 15-20, we held the first medical seminar since the hostage crisis. We had forty medical workers attend. They were struggling with hurt feelings. We needed to talk through some misunderstandings. When the opportunity was given after one of our morning messages, the Holy Spirit came down, and there was a spontaneous response. Darianus, leader of the Nduga medical work, took the lead. The confession and repentance that followed was like a popcorn meeting as the Holy Spirit moved in almost everyone's life."

Rebel In the Night

With every step of encouragement, a new countermove by the enemy blocked the path.

"When Larry Fish, our Field Director from Jakarta was visiting us in the Mbuwa with his wife, Carol, we had a crisis of sorts. That evening, after the light had gone out, there was a knock on our door. There stood Silas, a rebel Nduga leader. I made it clear that I could not see him and shut the door. It would raise suspicion in a fluid rebel situation. Elfrieda spent a prayerful night since we had houseguests. Nothing confrontational happened that night, but we agreed that we should leave the Mbuwa the following day. Kelly Kwalik, the head of the revolutionary rebellion, was nearby. Despite bad weather, MAF was able to fly us out. After we left the Mbuwa, we were involved in an evangelistic seminar at Pyramid."

There was no time to waste. Adriaan and Elfrieda moved from Pyramid on to Timika where Adriaan never misses a beat.

"While in Timika, I had the opportunity to minister with the evangelistic team in three church areas and four transmigrant camps. I went out every evening showing the Jesus film and The Ten Commandments which were drawing cards to attract people. Both Papuan and transmigrants from other islands made decisions for Christ. Pastor Agus, a Javanese evangelist who grew up in Papua, has received a real vision for the migrant camps."

Where Adriaan saw a need that was larger than his capacity, God provided a Javanese man with a vision for the migrant camps and beyond. Pastor Agus is still having a fruitful ministry and reaching out to the villages beyond Timika.

"Shockingly, the time is speeding by with only one full year left before we leave this wonderful land and people. Many missionary journeys are needed. With twelve major valleys and more than seventy churches, it is an insurmountable task. But we trust we can visit at least some of the valleys. To do this, we will have to use the helicopter extensively."

Adriaan and Elfrieda witnessed signs everywhere that God is in control and is going before his servant. Every step, every town, every landing seemed like a God-moment.

"On a high note, we flew to Bali for the Indonesian Field Forum which included all the C&MA missionaries across Indonesia. Returning to Papua from Bali, we had a brief stop in Timika before going onto Sentani. I met with the highest military commander in Papua who gave us his full support in our efforts to minister to the Ndugas."

Adriaan and Elfrieda moved from station to station, and in every place, there was another indication of the enduring fruit of the Lord's work. The tapestry was unfolding.

"Three days later we were in Wamena. It was exciting for us to attend the graduation of 154 nurses, all dressed in white. It was rewarding to see fourteen of our Nduga medical workers, who had completed the government correspondence course, graduating with them."

Everywhere there were footprints of God's guiding in their work, for which Adriaan was thankful. He was still solving problems and projecting coming events.

> "While in Wamena, we were busy visiting in government offices, meeting people to settle problems, and discussing future plans. It was a relief to get back to the Mbuwa, our haven of rest, away from the hustle and bustle of the big cities."

Adriaan stepped out the door the next morning into another opportunity. Government officials from Wamena had come to train some of their young Nduga men for civil service.

> "While one day our young Ndugas were dressed only in gourds, the next day they marched around in military uniforms. These men are being trained to keep the peace in their villages. I was given the occasion to give spiritual input. What a God-given opportunity. In front of me sat a whole group of military men, mostly from the other Indonesian islands as well as the government official. I told them that it does not matter who we are, or what we have done, God gave his Son the Lord Jesus as Saviour for all mankind, and that his love is unconditional and eternal.
>
> Elfrieda was given a full morning to teach and give practical hands-on instruction in first aid measures to prepare them for medical emergencies, such as landslides, earthquakes or fires."

The avalanche of opportunities was taking its toll on Adriaan. He admitted he was beginning to find the demands of travel and ministry quite challenging physically and emotionally.

The Pyramid Seminar

An evangelistic seminar in the Baliem Valley was needed to prepare workers to reach into unreached lowland areas toward the north coast. Adriaan and Elfrieda were involved.

> "We planned a Mamberamo Road Outreach Seminar for Pyramid.

While the great '97 drought raged all around us, nothing could deter the twelve men who were chosen to follow medical instructions given by Elfrieda. After holding a seminar in March for about one hundred evangelists, we held a follow-up seminar in September. These men had volunteered to invade new areas along the Mamberamo Road being built between Jayapura and Wamena."

Adriaan began the day teaching from the Book of Joshua. Elfrieda had the rest of the day to present a thorough drill of the fundamental principles of health, hygiene, medicines, treatment, and good common sense.

"You cannot make full-fledged medical workers in ten days. Yet the Lord gave us intelligent and eager men with at least high school and some Bible training."

Alpius, showing leadership as an evangelistic coordinator, told of some miraculous happenings which earned them the favour of the road crews.

"A huge boulder would not budge for the road crew. Alpius and his team prayed about it that night. The next day the big rock rolled away with very little effort. Later a road crew was unable to cross a river.

Again, the evangelistic team prayed, and the river dried up in two days. The road crew said they could not have made the progress they were making without the presence of the evangelists. They made the road camp available to them for their ministry. Miraculously God opened another door for his Word to be proclaimed."

The Decision

It was a shock to Adriaan and Elfrieda when Larry Fish, their C&MA Field Director, visiting from Jakarta, Java suggested that they should consider going home early, after the July 1998 Field Conference. John Wilson, the Papua C&MA leader from Jayapura, was with him.

"He came on quite strong saying that he sensed I was at the end of my rope, more or less.

We had already made up our minds to stay until the end of the year. It will involve not getting my re-entry visa. I will likely lose it. I do not feel worn out, although I cannot take pressure as well anymore. Elfrieda has felt that I was burned out for some time since she lives the closest to me.

My reactions to certain situations are not as they were, and I admit that. Not being able to cope with little and big things. Now we have only two months left!"

The stress of the international hostage incident left Adriaan with lingering health issues that affected his immune system critically. It weakened and affected a giant of a man. The hostage-taking amid all that needed to be done crippled his ability to say goodbye. It is not strange that this should be so. It is not strange that the Ndugas mourned his retirement. The sadness was accompanied by weeping that was mutual. What held them steady was that the God who led them so specifically throughout the years would continue to be their guiding light.

The Sum of a Ministry

It is time to try to sum up a life.

If we begin with the givens of Adriaan's ministry, we would have to say that beyond the dogged persistence and unremitting resilience in the face of struggle, what characterized Adriaan from beginning to end was his love of teaching. He was a natural and gifted teacher. Wherever he went, he ended up in the classroom where he felt most at home.

It was sad that it ended before they could prepare for it to end. But for Adriaan and Elfrieda, the impromptu last-minute goodbye coronations were what they needed.

"The Ndugas in Timika asked for a farewell celebration. They picked us up by taxi. Ndugas lined the road dressed like they had been when we arrived years ago. The girls wore black grass skirts, some with white bras, others with black, and decorated with white flower designs. The fellows were blackened up and wearing feather headdresses. There must have been about 1,000 strong.

They came running toward us complete with spears and the occasional bow and arrows. The police were there, just in case. After picture taking, we joined in the celebration. It was on the level of pomp that Princess Di would draw. It was a wonderful culmination.

It is hard for the Ndugas to face reality and for us, too. When everyone settled down, we sang several songs. I had a special message for them, a reminder of how it used to be and what the Lord has miraculously done. I told them that they should keep looking to the Lord who will never leave them.

Then they served sweet potatoes, greens, pork and chicken. It was a gigantic feast. People were sad, yet warm in their goodbyes. Everyone wanted to shake our hands. It was our first farewell gathering. Now several want to come to Mbuwa for the grand finale.

The Mbuwa Ndugas prepared an impressive send-off. While the pigs and garden produce were steaming in the pits, they put on a beautiful farewell program. Special farewell songs were composed for the occasion and sung by the youth. Touching speeches of their grateful thankfulness for bringing the gospel to them touched our hearts. They gave us hand-crafted net bags and strings of Nduga beads."

Rev. Arie Verduijn with the Alliance World Fellowship was visiting at the time. He had a message for the Nduga people based on Exodus 39. He told them how God clothed the priests with garments reflecting his glory and beauty. The high priest's breastplate was worn over his heart and featured twelve colourful gemstones, one for each of the names of the sons of Israel. Arie Verduijn assured them that Jesus would continue to carry each one by name on his heart and continually intercede for them. Besides that, on the shoulders of the high priests were two onyx stones which were engraved with the twelve names of the tribes of Israel.

So, Jesus will carry them on his shoulders. There is no need to fear because he promised never to leave them. His message was dynamic, full of hope and comfort to reassure the Ndugas that the presence of the Lord would remain with them despite their beloved missionaries leaving.

"These precious friends in Christ opened their hearts to us with such love, devotion and grateful thanks for the years we had spent with them. The memories of sitting by the fires in their huts and getting insight into their lives flash through our minds. The satisfying reward of being surrounded by them on that celebration day will never be forgotten."

It is not surprising that Adriaan and Elfrieda's last hurrah and final gesture to the people they loved would be to throw them a party, van der Bijl style. They engineered a fooddrop to the Ndugas as their send-off.

> "We have come up with the grandiose idea of bringing in twenty tons of food. As explained, our area is a red area because of the hostage-taking and can only be helped by the International Red Cross where there is military personnel present, and MAF service in the other places. So we have to be there in that village where everything will be dropped by huge Australian Air Force helicopters here at the moment helping out. They can move about two tons or 4,000 pounds per flight, whereas the little MAF helicopters can only move about 550 pounds per flight. Because of the political hassle we have been under, the flights cost us nothing, so we will be there to coordinate this."

Never Again the Last Cucumber on the Vine

There's a little *kopi* fruit that grows in the Papua valleys—similar to squash in North America—that tastes like cucumber. It's not plentiful, like the ever-present sweet potatoes that make up the Nduga diet, but to them, it is a symbol of essential nourishment. When they spoke of the last cucumber on the vine, it meant more than a sense of being left out. It was a symbol of survival, of life itself.

Many times in their history the Nduga tribe suffered starvation. The thought that there would be no fruit on the vine was a daily possibility. They lived with the stark reality that they would look through their gardens and discover that they had picked the last cucumber on the vine.

The gospel message of a life-giving vine that flourishes and never withers give new meaning to the Nduga future. And though the van der Bijls were leaving, Jesus will always be with them. Never again would the Ndugas be the last cucumber on the vine. One of the last words the Ndugas expressed still comforts and reassures them in the night. These words are riveted in their memories forever:

"It is hard to say goodbye. But Jesus is with us. We'll be OK."

64320822R00139

Made in the USA
Middletown, DE
02 September 2019